MATT TEBBUTT'S
PUB
FOOD

MATT TEBBUTT'S
PUB
FOOD

100 Favourites, Old and New

Photography by Chris Terry

quadrille

CONTENTS

INTRODUCTION

Ever since I can remember, pubs have been a part of my life. From the early days of a lemonade and packet of crisps in a quiet corner of the bar, via half a shandy and chicken in a basket in the beer garden, through to the life-affirming rite of passage that is ordering your first pint and enjoying a good lean on the bar with everyone else.

A great pub is something a bit special in life. Visits can be impromptu, or planned, and you can walk in alone or with a crowd. You go to the pub in all sorts of moods – to celebrate, to chill out, to commiserate. Pubs are open to everyone, very few places are as universally welcoming. There's no pressure walking into a local pub, not like there is with a cutting-edge restaurant or swanky bar. There's no pomp or pretension. Pubs are a welcoming safe space, somewhere to sit alone with your own thoughts or hold court in a crowd. Nobody cares either way and no one will judge you.

In my experience, the best pubs are accessible to all, the last genuine melting pots of society, where old and young, rich and poor can mingle at ease. A good pub is a home from home, somewhere you can speak your mind surrounded by friends, strangers, comics and even bores! A great pub should feel well lived in and, like the best people, a bit shabby around the edges, clean but not overly polished.

I spend a fair amount of time in pubs and in my opinion, a pub should be value for money and have a warmth and charm in all of its mismatched crockery, a saggy sofa or two and eclectic bric-a-brac hanging on the walls and ceilings. The best places are intimate and cosy with low lighting, all making it feel instantly comfortable and relaxing.

Good, well-renowned boozers have always prided themselves on the quality and selection of beer and spirits they offer, but these days many of them are also looking to provide the same standards with their food offering. I like pub food without any pretensions or fancy garnishes. Dishes can be modern and original, but should always be found alongside the old, more familiar crowd-pleasing classics that put the diner at ease.

Honest and approachable flavours are key to a great pub menu as well as access to the best and freshest local produce. There must be robust and delicious flavours, with interesting and sometimes unusual dishes. The phrase 'bold flavours and rough edges' was coined by one of the first gastropub pathfinders David Eyre at The Eagle in Farringdon in London, which was established in 1991 and went on to be the blueprint for so many other chefs, including me, to follow.

There's been something of a revolution since then and most pub food has changed beyond recognition in the past 30 years. One of the big benefits is the focus on locally sourced produce and regional dishes. Local produce is heartily celebrated by chefs and customers alike and is reflected in menus across the country.

When we set The Foxhunter up in 2000, the catchphrase 'seasonal and local' wasn't really a thing. Chefs were used to getting their vegetables delivered from the mega markets of Europe and all the meat and fish largely arrived in the kitchen in plastic-wrapped containers, cut and ready to sell, origin often unknown. And during the 90s this was common practice in all manner of restaurants, from the most basic to fine dining. Food provenance was not the order of the day.

When we moved from central London to rural Monmouthshire, it just made sense. It made sense to buy from the local farms, it made sense to buy what was only available locally and in season – it made sense for our kitchen budget and it made sense on the menu. We were lucky, of course, with the quality and range of the local produce here in Wales and in the borders.

It seemed crazy to be importing all sorts of produce from overseas when we had so much right in front of us. The menu had a real purpose and a true sense of seasonality. The locals loved the idea of knowing where their food came from in a way the city diner never seemed to worry about it in those days. It connected the chefs and the restaurant to where we were, and it paid dividends.

I loved our daily changing menu, it gave me so much flexibility and I could react to what was coming in through the kitchen door. Sometimes a seasonal glut would arrive, like the first of the new season's wild garlic or a few handfuls of rare autumnal porcini. I loved having the ability to quickly rewrite the menu to make the most of whatever was on offer and this is what modern pubs are good at, because they are small and flexible.

A good kitchen excels and revels in this. It's spontaneous and fun for everyone – kitchen and customer. And this is what I loved about owning a pub, the freedom of choice that I had and imparted onto the menu, a spontaneity that no busy city restaurant could offer.

There is often more of a direct connection between a country pub kitchen and the local surroundings than any high-end city restaurant could imagine. Local farmers and producers supply these kitchens with great quality, fresh, seasonal produce all year round – all essential to delivering great food to the customer.

In 2003 the brilliant food writer Diana Henry, wrote that pubs are Britain's 'brasseries and bistros' and that they are here to stay. There's no doubt that well-trained chefs who wanted to get out the Michelin-starred kitchens of London and beyond to follow their own dreams in a more simple and relaxed fashion, have made a real impact on dining out in this country. Many, like me, saw snapping up a local boozer as the most economical way of doing this. The term gastropub was hijacked along the way by bigger corporate enterprises and the term has somewhat fallen out of favour. What has endured however, is the legacy that throughout the land, good pubs can offer a warm welcome, a great pint and some of the best food you'll find anywhere.

As the great hotelier and restaurateur Kit Chapman once said, 'the battle for an improvement in British dining would be won or lost in its pubs' and he was right.

I hope you enjoy this selection of recipes influenced by my time owning, drinking in and working in pubs.

SOUPS, STARTERS & LIGHT LUNCHES

WHITE ONION SOUP WITH CHICKEN LIVERS AND GARLIC CRISPS

I do like soups with interesting 'bits' in. If you're not with me on the combinations, then feel free to omit the offending elements, or try substituting other flavours. The soup is silky and delicious on its own, not at all overpowering as might be expected. Serve with a bottle of rich red wine and lots of warm crusty bread.

SERVES 4

3 large white onions, peeled
    and diced
2 bay leaves
2 sprigs fresh thyme, leaves picked
50g unsalted butter
2 tbsp olive oil
3 garlic cloves, peeled and
    roughly chopped
1 large baking potato, peeled
    and diced
1 litre chicken or vegetable stock
    (see pages 222 or 220), or water
200ml double cream
salt and pepper
6–8 chicken livers
10g salted butter
crusty bread, to serve

FOR THE GARLIC CRISPS
olive oil
4 garlic cloves, peeled and cut
    into slivers
1 sprig fresh thyme
sea salt flakes

In a saucepan, sweat the onions, bay leaves and most of the thyme in 40g of the butter and the oil until the onions are soft but not coloured, about 10 minutes. Throw in the garlic, stir and cover, and cook gently for another 10 minutes, checking from time to time to prevent burning. Add the diced potato and stir together for 5 minutes.

Pour in the stock or water and bring to the boil. Cook for 20 minutes or until all the ingredients are soft. Add the cream and return to the boil. Remove from the heat and blend with the remaining unsalted butter. Push through a fine sieve. Season to taste.

For the garlic crisps, gently heat up enough oil to cover the base of a small pan. Throw in the garlic slivers and thyme, and cook until golden brown. Remove the garlic with a slotted spoon and drain on kitchen paper. Season with salt flakes and set aside somewhere warm.

Season the chicken livers with salt, pepper and the remaining thyme leaves. Fry them off in a little salted butter until rare, about 2 minutes, as the heat of the soup will continue their cooking. Slice the livers in half.

Pour the soup into warmed bowls, top each with 2 liver halves and sprinkle over the garlic crisps.

TUSCAN BEAN SOUP

This traditional Italian soup is known as ribollita. It's the perfect way to
warm up on a cold day – comfort food at its best.

SERVES 4

FOR THE BEANS
200g dried broad beans,
    soaked overnight
200g dried white beans,
    soaked overnight
1 onion, peeled and chopped
1 carrot, peeled and chopped
1 celery stick, chopped
300g unsmoked pancetta with rind
1 sprig rosemary
2 garlic cloves, peeled and
    left whole

FOR THE SOUP BASE
2 tbsp olive oil, plus extra
    for drizzling
1 onion, peeled and diced
1 carrot, peeled and diced
2 celery sticks, diced
3 garlic cloves, peeled and minced
1 sprig rosemary
2 bay leaves
1 potato, peeled and diced
½ turnip, peeled and diced
500ml vegetable stock

TO SERVE
1 head of cavolo nero, roughly
    chopped and blanched
4 slices day-old sourdough bread
50g Parmesan, freshly grated

Place the beans in a large casserole or saucepan with the onion, carrot, celery, pancetta, rosemary and garlic and cover with water. Cook over a gentle heat for 1½–2 hours or until the beans are soft. Leave to cool in the cooking liquid. Sieve the beans into a bowl, reserving the cooking liquid, then pick out the pancetta and shred. Discard the cooked veg and herbs.

Preheat the oven to 180°C/350°F/Gas 4.

To make the soup base, heat the oil in a large ovenproof casserole and sweat the onion, carrot, celery and garlic for 10 minutes. Add the rosemary, bay leaves, potato and turnip to the casserole and fry for a couple of minutes.

Tip the beans, pancetta and their cooking liquid into the casserole. Add enough of the vegetable stock to just cover the soup. Cover with a lid and cook in the oven for 1 hour. Top up with more stock if needed. Remove the casserole from the oven but leave the oven on.

Pick out the herbs and purée half of the soup in a blender or food processor, then mix into the unblended half. Stir in the cavolo nero.

Ladle a third of the soup into a large ovenproof dish and top with half of the bread. Ladle over more soup, then the remaining bread. Ladle over the rest of the soup, sprinkle over the Parmesan and drizzle over a generous glug of olive oil. Bake for 30–40 minutes or until it forms a crust. Serve in warmed soup bowls.

TOMATO, BREAD AND BASIL SOUP

Traditional recipes always seem to be the best. This soup was a means of using up leftover bread and making the most of the abundant tomatoes and fabulous local olive oil. Many European countries have an equivalent, and I first discovered something similar in Portugal.

It's best made with the ripest tomatoes and the stalest bread, and please don't scrimp on the quality of the olive oil. This is a light, summery treat.

SERVES 4-6

extra virgin olive oil
2 tsp chopped fresh sage leaves
4 garlic cloves, peeled and cut
    into slivers
10 fresh tomatoes, skinned
    and chopped
400g can plum tomatoes
4 slices stale ciabatta or sourdough
    bread, 2.5cm thick
salt and pepper
1 litre stock (vegetable or chicken,
    see pages 220 and 222)
1 bunch fresh basil
freshly shaved Parmesan

Heat up a big slug of olive oil in a large saucepan, throw in the sage, garlic and the fresh tomatoes and stir. Add the canned plum tomatoes and tear in the stale bread. Season.

Pour in the stock and simmer for 45 minutes. Stir frequently to break down the tomatoes and smooth out the soup.

Serve at room temperature topped with freshly torn basil, shaved Parmesan and plenty of extra virgin olive oil.

SWEETCORN SOUP WITH GIROLLES AND TARRAGON

This soup was always on my restaurant menu throughout September, with girolles and sweetcorn being great seasonal partners. Sautéed together, they make an excellent accompaniment to a very good piece of fish, such as turbot.

SERVES 4

2 onions, peeled and roughly
    chopped
½ head of celery, roughly chopped
50g unsalted butter
olive oil
3 sprigs fresh tarragon, leaves and
    stalks separated
2 bay leaves
salt and pepper
8 whole sweetcorn cobs, stripped
    of the corn
1 garlic bulb, cut in half
water or chicken stock (see
    page 222)
50g girolles or other wild
    mushrooms per person

In a frying pan, fry the onions and celery in the butter and 1 tablespoon or so of olive oil until soft. Add the tarragon stalks for flavour, plus the bay leaves. Season.

Throw in the corn and garlic, barely cover with water or chicken stock and simmer for 20–40 minutes until the corn is well cooked. Purée the soup in a blender and push through a sieve. Reserve.

Fry off the mushrooms in a little olive oil, and season with salt and pepper. Chuck in the finely chopped tarragon leaves. Heat the soup through and serve garnished with the mushrooms.

CHESTNUT AND BACON SOUP

A great winter soup, one of my favourites in fact. Chestnuts have a lovely
sweetness to them. It's quite a filling little number, what with the bacon
and Parmesan, so would be suitable as a supper dish in its own right.

SERVES 6-8

6–8 garlic cloves, peeled
   and crushed
1 large white onion, peeled
   and diced
2 carrots, diced
2 celery sticks, diced
50g salted butter
2 tsp olive oil
1 sprig fresh rosemary
salt and pepper
150g smoked bacon or pancetta,
   diced
1 tbsp tomato purée
500g prepared blanched chestnuts,
   roughly chopped
1 bay leaf
chicken stock (see page 222) or
   water, to cover

TO SERVE
extra virgin olive oil
freshly grated Parmesan

In a saucepan, sweat the garlic, onion, carrot and celery in the
butter and oil with the rosemary for 10 minutes. Season lightly.

Add the diced pancetta and continue to cook for a further 10 minutes.
Stir in the tomato purée and cook out for a further 2–3 minutes.
Add the chopped chestnuts and allow to cook for a few minutes.
Finally add the bay leaf and chicken stock (or water) and simmer
for 20–30 minutes. Check the seasoning.

Purée the soup in a blender, then pass through a sieve. Serve
with a good slug of quality extra virgin olive oil and some freshly
grated Parmesan.

CAULIFLOWER SOUP WITH BLACK PUDDING AND DILL

The black pudding and dill add some texture and colour to this seasonal soup.

SERVES 4-6

2 small cauliflowers
1 white onion, peeled and chopped
90g salted butter
1 sprig fresh thyme
2 garlic cloves, peeled and crushed
1 bunch fresh dill, fronds and
    stalks separated
1 bay leaf
milk, to cover
200g black pudding
2 shallots, peeled and finely chopped
salt and pepper

Cut out the stalks of the cauliflowers and grate the rest into a bowl.

In a saucepan, sweat the chopped onion in a third of the butter with the thyme, garlic and dill stalks for 10 minutes. Add the grated cauliflower and bay leaf, and sweat for a further 5 minutes. Cover with milk and simmer for 25 minutes.

Meanwhile, take the black pudding flesh out of the skins, break it down and mix with about 1 tablespoon of the chopped dill fronds and all the chopped shallots. Form into balls the size of an old penny. Pan-fry these balls in half the remaining butter for 8–10 minutes until cooked through and keep warm.

Season the cauliflower mixture to taste. Purée in a blender with the remaining cold butter and then pass through a fine sieve. Heat through, then portion into individual bowls. Place the black pudding balls in the soup and garnish with the remaining dill fronds.

TOMATOES AND MOZZARELLA ON BRIOCHE

This is my favourite snack. Proper fast food, it takes 10 minutes start to finish and is totally delicious just as long as the tomatoes are good quality and ripe and the mozzarella is super-fresh.

SERVES 2

25g salted butter
salt and pepper
4 plum or 2 beef tomatoes, the
    ripest and most flavoursome,
    sliced lengthways
4 anchovy fillets
120g crème fraîche
2 balls buffalo mozzarella, torn
    into pieces
a few basil leaves
2 slices large brioche loaf

Heat the butter in a frying pan until foaming, then season the tomatoes and sauté for 5 minutes or so. Turn the tomatoes over and cook for a further 5 minutes. Add the anchovy fillets and mash to dissolve.

Stir in the crème fraîche, then bring to the boil to thicken. Throw in the mozzarella, then add the basil. Stir two or three times and remove from the heat.

Toast the slices of brioche, and spoon the tomato and crème fraîche sauce over them. Serve immediately.

CAESAR SALAD

This recipe puts more of a British twist on the classic American recipe.

SERVES 4

2 red romaine lettuces,
   leaves separated
1 butterhead lettuce,
   leaves separated
2 slices white bread, cut into
   croutons and oven-baked or
   fried with garlic and thyme oil
100g Old Winchester cheese (or
   Parmesan), freshly grated
4 medium free-range eggs,
   soft-boiled and peeled

FOR THE DRESSING
3 medium free-range egg yolks
2 garlic cloves, peeled and crushed
1 tbsp Dijon mustard
salt and pepper
150ml olive oil
150ml vegetable oil
juice of ½ lemon
8–10 anchovy fillets
100g Old Winchester or Parmesan,
   freshly grated

In a mixer, make the dressing as for mayonnaise (see page 230), but stirring in the cheese and anchovies at the end. Taste and season with salt and pepper.

To assemble the dish, dress all the lettuce in a large bowl with the thick anchovy dressing. Throw in the croutons and a good amount of the grated cheese.

Pile everything onto a plate and break the soft-boiled eggs over the top. Add a little more grated cheese to serve.

SPINACH AND RICOTTA FLAN

I used not to have many go-to vegetarian dishes, but this is an Italian recipe I discovered while holidaying in Florence, and I really love it. Great texture and subtle flavours. I like to pair this with a good mozzarella or burrata and some roasted cherry tomatoes, or melt some Gorgonzola over the top.

SERVES 6-8

unsalted butter, for greasing
1kg fresh spinach
250g ricotta cheese
2 medium free-range eggs
100g Parmesan, freshly grated
freshly grated nutmeg
70ml extra virgin olive oil
salt and pepper

TO SERVE
1 large bag of rocket
pine nuts, toasted

Preheat the oven to 160°C/325°F/Gas 3, and grease a medium, about 20cm, springform flan tin with butter.

Quickly blanch the spinach in boiling salted water. Drain, squeeze it dry and chop quite finely.

In a bowl stir all the ingredients together, and season. Using a stick blender or food processor, blitz the ingredients together. You should now have a green pulp that slightly resembles baby food.

Pour the mixture into the prepared tin, and bake in the preheated oven for 5 minutes until crisp looking. Turn the temperature down to 100°C/210°F/Gas ¼, and continue to cook for another 30–40 minutes. Remove and leave to cool a little.

Serve warm or at room temperature with some rocket leaves and toasted pine nuts.

FOIL-BAKED WILD MUSHROOMS

Use the best-looking ceps or other wild mushrooms you've picked, or shopped for, as they will be the sole focus of the dish. Mop up the juices with plenty of fresh bread or soft polenta and grated Parmesan.

SERVES 2

150–200g fresh ceps or other
    wild mushrooms
2–3 bay leaves
2–3 sprigs fresh thyme
sea salt flakes and black pepper
50ml olive oil
1 garlic clove, peeled and
    finely sliced
finely grated zest of 1 unwaxed
    lemon

TO SERVE
bread or soft polenta
freshly grated Parmesan

Preheat the oven to 200–220°C/400–425°F/Gas 6–7.

Brush the mushrooms, but do not wash them. Put in a foil square with the rest of the ingredients. Seal up the parcel and bake in a shallow pan of water (to prevent scorching) in the oven for 20 minutes or so.

Serve immediately. The mushrooms should be just softening but still have bite.

SMOKED HADDOCK SOUFFLÉ TART

Lighter than a traditional quiche, but just as satisfying. Always source naturally smoked haddock.

SERVES 4

2 smoked haddock fillets
1.5 litres whole milk
1 bunch fresh dill, chopped
60g unsalted butter, melted
50g strong Cheddar, grated
1 tbsp crème fraîche or
    double cream
3 free-range eggs, separated
1 ready-made 22cm round
    shortcrust pastry case
salt and pepper

TO SERVE
mixed green salad dressed with
    olive oil and lemon juice
lemon wedges

Preheat the oven to 200°C/400°F/Gas 6.

Place the haddock and milk in a large saucepan and poach for 8–10 minutes or until cooked through.

Remove the fish, leave to cool and break the haddock into flakes. Place the haddock in a bowl and stir in the dill, melted butter, cheese and crème fraîche and season with salt and pepper. Add the egg yolks and mix to combine.

In a separate bowl, whisk the whites until stiff peaks form. Fold the egg whites gently through the haddock mixture. Spoon the haddock mixture into the tart shell and bake for 35 minutes or until the filling has risen and the pastry is golden.

Serve the tart in slices with a green salad, and a lemon wedge for squeezing over.

FRIED CUTTLEFISH WITH CHILLI BUTTER

This is a Sri Lankan-inspired recipe. Crispy deep-fried cuttlefish, nice and spicy, with a lovely nutty flavour from the brown butter. Cuttlefish is found all around the UK, but you can use squid the same way.

SERVES 2

FOR THE FRIED CUTTLEFISH
4 small cuttlefish, cleaned
1 free-range egg white
a pinch of salt, plus 1 tsp
1 tsp ground turmeric
oil, for deep-frying
100g cornflour
1 tbsp black pepper

FOR THE CHILLI BUTTER
100g unsalted butter
1–2 tbsp chilli paste or chilli flakes
4 garlic cloves, peeled and
   finely chopped

TO SERVE
6 spring onions, chopped
1 lime, cut into wedges

Cut the cuttlefish into small chunks. Put the egg white in a bowl and mix in the pinch of salt and the turmeric. Marinate the cuttlefish in the egg white for 10 minutes.

Preheat a deep-fat fryer or a wok of oil to 180°C/350°F.

Mix the cornflour, the teaspoon of salt and the black pepper together and toss the cuttlefish in the seasoned flour.

Carefully lower the cuttlefish into the hot oil to deep-fry for a few minutes, or until crisp and golden brown. Remove using a slotted spoon onto a plate lined with kitchen paper. Leave in a warm place.

Melt the butter in a pan over a medium heat and cook until it reaches a nut-brown colour, then add the chilli paste or flakes and the garlic.

To serve, toss the cuttlefish in the butter and add the spring onions. Serve with lime wedges.

SQUID MARINIERE WITH SALT AND VINEGAR COCKLES

A nice change from mussels, this makes a great bar snack or light lunch.
Clams work just as well if cockles aren't available.

SERVES 2

FOR THE COCKLES
250g cockles in shell
50ml white wine
1 tbsp fine sea salt
2 tbsp malt vinegar
2 tbsp plain flour
100ml milk
oil, for frying
salt and pepper

FOR THE SQUID
15g salted butter
1 shallot, peeled and diced
2 garlic cloves, peeled and
    finely chopped
1 tsp chopped fresh thyme
1 bay leaf
50ml white wine
50ml double cream
4 medium squid, cut into thin rings
1 squeeze lemon juice
a handful of chopped fresh parsley

Give the cockles a rinse to wash away any sand or dirt. If any of the cockle shells are open, tap them against a hard surface, which should encourage them to close. If the shell remains open, discard the cockle.

Heat a large saucepan, add the cockles and wine and put a lid on. Cook over a hight heat until the cockles open. They should cook within a few minutes and the shells will open. Any that do not open should be discarded. Drain the liquid and set it aside, then pick the meat from the cockles and set aside separately. Discard the shells.

Put the salt and vinegar in a pan and cook until all the vinegar has evaporated. Set aside.

For the squid, heat the butter in a pan and add the shallot, garlic, thyme and bay leaf. Gently fry for a few minutes. Add the white wine and cook until reduced in thickness, then pour in the reserved cockle liquid and reduce to taste. Keep warm.

To finish the cockles, sprinkle the flour onto a plate and season with salt and freshly ground black pepper. Pour the milk into a small bowl. Dip the cockles in the milk, followed by the seasoned flour. Heat a dash of oil in a pan and fry the cockles until crisp and golden brown on all sides. Remove from the pan, sprinkle over the salt and vinegar mixture and keep warm.

To finish the squid, add the cream to the mix, bring to a boil, throw in the squid, turn the heat right down and cook for a minute until opaque and cooked through. Remove from the heat. Taste, season with salt, and add the lemon juice and parsley. Sprinkle the cockles over the squid and serve.

PORTUGUESE SALT COD CAKES

Working in London exposes you to many interesting characters. In one restaurant, the pot-washer would bang on about his cooking skills being much better than those of us mere chefs. He gave us his recipe for salt cod cakes and, in all their simplicity, they may well prove he was right.

SERVES 4-6

2 white onions, peeled and
    finely diced
3 garlic cloves, peeled and
    finely chopped
olive oil
600g salt cod
500ml milk
1 bay leaf
2 sprigs fresh thyme
400g freshly cooked mashed potato
    (see page 153)
3 medium free-range egg yolks
a handful of chopped fresh
    flat-leaf parsley
salt and pepper
vegetable oil, for deep-frying
plain flour
lemon wedges, to serve
garlic mayonnaise (aïoli, see
    page 41), to serve

In a saucepan, sweat the diced onion and garlic in some olive oil for 10 minutes. Set aside.

Meanwhile, in another pan, poach the salt cod in the milk with the bay leaf and thyme, until just cooked and able to be flaked, about 5–6 minutes. Remove the fish from the milk and flake into the mashed potato with the egg yolks and parsley. Fold in the onion and garlic, then check for seasoning. Shape into small 50p-sized balls, and chill to firm up.

When ready to cook, heat the vegetable oil to 170°C/325°F in a deep-fat fryer or wok, coat the cod cakes in a light dusting of flour and deep-fry for 5–6 minutes until golden and hot in the middle. Check this by inserting a knife into the centre – it should come out very hot. If not, put the cod cakes back in the oil or warm in a hot oven for a few minutes.

Serve the cod cakes with nothing more than a wedge of lemon and some garlic mayonnaise, if liked.

SOUSED HERRING, PICKLED CUCUMBER AND CRÈME FRAÎCHE

Soused herring is a great standby as it keeps exceptionally well in the fridge and makes a perfect light lunch or supper dish. The important thing is to use herrings at their best.

SERVES 4

6 shallots, peeled and finely sliced
   into half-moons
sea salt
olive oil
1 tsp mixed peppercorns
1 star anise
a few parsley stalks
2 sprigs fresh thyme
100ml white wine
50ml white wine vinegar
200ml salad oil (half vegetable,
   half olive) or neutral tasting oil
   (such as peanut)
8 herring fillets, pin-boned
4 tsp crème fraîche, to serve

**FOR THE PICKLED
CUCUMBER**

2 cucumbers
sea salt
400ml white wine vinegar
100g caster sugar, plus extra to
   taste if necessary
½ bunch fresh dill or chervil
   or tarragon, chopped

Season the shallots with salt and sauté gently in a frying pan with a splash of olive oil for 5 minutes, just to take the edge off. Add the aromatics, white wine, white wine vinegar and salad oil. Bring to a gentle simmer and remove from the heat.

Lay the fillets of raw herring in a tray and pour over the marinade. The marinade must be hot, as the acidity of the marinade coupled with the gentle heat will cook the fish very delicately. Cover the baking tray and allow to cool naturally.

Meanwhile for the pickled cucumber, slice the cucumbers from head to toe, removing the seeds with a spoon. Slice them finely, preferably using a mandoline, about 2mm in width. Put into a colander and season heavily with sea salt. Leave for 1 hour to drain. Squeeze the excess moisture from the cucumber with a clean tea towel and set aside.

Heat the white wine vinegar and sugar together in a saucepan until the sugar has dissolved. Taste and add more sugar if necessary. There should be a nice balance between acidity and sweetness. Pour over the cucumber, add the chopped herb of your choice and leave to marinate for half an hour or more.

Serve the pickled herrings along with the cucumber and some good-quality crème fraîche.

SALT COD, ARTICHOKE AND AÏOLI

This is best served warm or at room temperature. Essentially it is a pared-down 'le grand aïoli' — which for me is mainly a great excuse to make homemade aïoli.

SERVES 4

1 thick fillet of cod, no less than 1kg
lots of sea salt
extra virgin olive oil
6 baby globe artichokes, cut in half
    and blanched for 10–12 minutes
150g best-quality black or
    green olives
4 free-range eggs, boiled for 5–6
    minutes until just set
flat-leaf parsley and lemon wedges,
    to serve

FOR THE AÏOLI

3 garlic cloves, peeled and
    finely crushed
2 medium free-range eggs
salt and white pepper
250ml extra virgin olive oil
juice of 1 lemon

Put the cod in a dish and cover with a heavy seasoning of sea salt. Cover and leave overnight in the fridge.

Preheat the oven to 180°C/350°F/Gas 4.

To make the aïoli, put the crushed garlic in a bowl with the eggs and some salt and white pepper. Start to whisk, gradually adding the olive oil. Whisk until all the oil is in, and the sauce is thick. Let it down with enough lemon juice to taste. Reserve.

Quickly rinse off the salted cod fillet and pat dry. Heat a non-stick frying pan over a medium heat. Add some oil and pan-fry the cod, flesh-side down, until golden brown, 3–4 minutes. Turn the fish over and put into the preheated oven until cooked through, about 5 minutes. Test with the point of a knife: if it goes in without resistance it's ready. Keep the fish warm.

Toss the well-drained artichokes and olives in some good olive oil, and season.

To assemble the dish, lay the fish flesh-side up, top with halves of boiled egg and the artichokes and olives scattered over. Garnish with flat-leaf parsley and a lemon wedge, and serve with aïoli on the side.

SARDINES AND CARAMELISED ONION TART

This dish is great fun to make and looks really dramatic. It doesn't usually manage to reach the table whole, as everyone just starts digging in with their fingers.

SERVES 4

flour, for dusting
500g fresh or frozen puff pastry
4 large onions, peeled, halved
  and finely sliced
50ml olive oil
a few fresh thyme sprigs,
  leaves picked
salt and pepper
1 large tbsp olives, stoned and
  roughly chopped
10 fresh sardine fillets, pin-boned,
  heads removed but tails intact
flat-leaf parsley, to garnish

On a floured surface, roll out the puff pastry to a 30cm circle, transfer to a floured baking sheet, then fold over the edges and press with your fingers to make a rustic looking crimped edge, about 3mm thick. Prick with a fork all over and put in the fridge to chill.

In a frying pan, caramelise the onions slowly over a very low heat in the olive oil – this will take 1–1½ hours. Add the thyme and then salt and pepper at the end to season. Set aside.

Preheat the oven to 200°C/400°F/Gas 6.

Cook the puff pastry base in the preheated oven for 15 minutes or so until golden brown.

Remove from the oven and spread over the onions and a few thyme sprigs, leaving a border of pastry all round, avoiding the crimped edge. Sprinkle over the olives and arrange the sardines in a circle like the spokes of a wheel. Bake for 20 minutes or so until the sardines are cooked through. Remove from the oven and garnish with parsley. Cut into thick wedges to serve.

BLOODY MARY OYSTER SHOTS

The perfect hair of the dog, but I don't tend to wait for the morning after.

SERVES 2

6 rock oysters, opened and
   juices reserved
1 splash sherry (fino)
a pinch of celery salt

FOR THE BLOODY MARY MIX
1 splash Tabasco sauce
1 splash Worcestershire sauce
1 splash vodka
150ml tomato juice

Make the mix as for a Bloody Mary.

Lay an oyster into a shot glass. Cover with Bloody Mary mix, then add a splash of sherry, some of the reserved oyster juice and a pinch of celery salt.

Down in one!

CRAB AND CITRUS SALAD WITH CRISPBREADS

I like to make this crab salad as a sharing dish or pre-starter. The crispbreads are a dinner party show-off, but you could always buy in some nice quality ones.

SERVES 2

FOR THE CRAB SALAD
200g white crab meat
1 tbsp olive oil
1 lime, peeled and chopped
1 pink grapefruit, peeled
    and chopped
½ Braeburn apple, peeled
    and finely diced
salt and pepper

FOR THE DRESSING
2 tbsp brown crab meat
1 tbsp crème fraîche
juice of 1 lime

FOR THE CRISPBREADS
200g strong bread flour
7g sachet dried yeast
1 tsp sea salt
1 tbsp olive oil
1 tsp coriander seeds, toasted
    and crushed

TO SERVE
1 tbsp chopped fresh dill
1 tbsp chopped fresh tarragon

Mix the white crab meat with the olive oil in a large bowl and season with salt and pepper. Stir in the lime, grapefruit and apple.

For the dressing, place all of the ingredients in a food processor and blitz to a smooth paste. Transfer to a small bowl.

For the crispbreads, put the flour, yeast, salt and oil in a food processor with a dough hook attachment. Gradually add 100–150ml water until a dough is formed. Put in a bowl, cover with a tea towel and leave to prove for 1–2 hours, or until doubled in volume.

Preheat the oven to 220°C/425°F/Gas 7. Divide the dough into four and roll out each piece through a pasta machine on its thinnest setting, or roll by hand as thin as you dare. Lay on a baking tray, sprinkle over the crushed coriander seeds and some salt and brush over some oil. Cook for 8–10 minutes.

To serve, put the crispbreads on a serving plate. Spoon the dressing over the crispbreads, add the crab salad and garnish with the herbs.

Wysis Way

MONMOUTH

GRIDDLED TUNA WITH OLIVE TAPENADE AND GARLIC SOUP

I love this Mediterranean-style tuna dish. The silky garlic soup, fresh basil dressing and tapenade make for the perfect light lunch.

SERVES 2

200g tuna steak

FOR THE SOUP
2 tbsp olive oil
1 onion, peeled and diced
10 garlic cloves, peeled and
    chopped
2 potatoes, peeled and diced
1 bay leaf
500ml light chicken stock
100ml double cream
salt and pepper

FOR THE BLACK OLIVE
TAPENADE
100g black Kalamata olives,
    stones removed
2 garlic cloves, peeled and minced
2 anchovy fillets, roughly chopped
1 tsp chopped fresh thyme
50ml olive oil, to loosen
1 splash red wine vinegar

FOR THE BASIL DRESSING
1 bunch basil
150–200ml olive oil

TO SERVE
2 tbsp vegetable oil
2 garlic cloves, peeled and
    thinly sliced

To make the soup, heat the oil in a large saucepan and sweat the onion and garlic for 20 minutes. Add the potatoes and bay leaf, continue to sweat for another 10 minutes and then add the stock. Simmer for 30 minutes until the vegetables have softened, then add the cream. Bring back to the boil, season with salt and pepper and blitz to a smooth purée in a food processor or with a hand blender. Keep warm.

To make the black olive tapenade, blitz all of the ingredients, except the oil and vinegar, in a food processor or blender to a paste, then loosen with the oil. Add the vinegar, taste and season with salt and pepper.

To make the basil dressing, blanch the basil in boiling water for 30 seconds, then remove and refresh in cold water. Drain and squeeze all the water out, place the basil in a blender with the oil and blend until smooth. Pass through a sieve and set aside.

To cook the tuna, heat a griddle pan over a high heat. Season the tuna with salt and pepper, then griddle on both sides until charred on the outside and rare inside, 3–4 minutes depending on the thickness of the steak. Leave to rest, then slice.

To serve, heat the vegetable oil in a small frying pan. Fry the garlic until golden brown. Spoon the soup into bowls and drizzle over the basil dressing, olive tapenade and fried garlic. Serve with the tuna.

THINLY *SLICED* PORK WITH TUNA DRESSING

This dish has been adapted from the traditional *vitello tonnato,* poached veal with tuna sauce. When we were left with half a roast loin of pork from evening service in the restaurant, we found it made a delicious light lunch when served the following day with either the reheated meat juices, some shaved Parmesan and a few salad leaves, or with this tuna dressing. The important thing here is to serve the meat at room temperature and to slice it incredibly thinly.

SERVES 1-2
(depending on quantity of pork; the sauce will keep for a few days)

leftover pork loin, shoulder or leg, bone removed
1 tbsp baby capers
salad leaves

FOR THE MEAT JUICES
a small pan of the meat cooking stock
1 tbsp Dijon mustard
1 garlic clove, peeled and crushed
1 splash sherry vinegar
a few fresh thyme leaves
1 splash extra virgin olive oil
salt and pepper

FOR THE TUNA DRESSING
2 medium free-range egg yolks
1 small can tuna fillet in oil, drained
1 anchovy fillet
½ garlic clove, peeled and crushed
200ml salad oil (half vegetable, half extra virgin olive)
1 squeeze lemon juice, to taste
milk

To make the meat juices, bring the reserved meat stock to the boil, then whisk in the Dijon mustard, garlic, sherry vinegar, thyme leaves and olive oil. Taste and adjust the seasoning as necessary. Keep warm.

To make the tuna dressing, blend the egg yolks, tuna, anchovy and garlic to a paste. Slowly add the salad oil in a thin stream until all nicely emulsified. Add a squeeze of lemon juice to taste. Let the dressing down with some milk to make a thin consistency.

To assemble the dish, slice the pork very, very thinly and layer over a large platter. Simply dress the meat with the juices and tuna dressing. Scatter the baby capers and a few good salad leaves over the top. Serve.

BLACK PUDDING, SMOKED EEL, CARAMELISED APPLES AND CIDER MUSTARD SAUCE

This recipe throws together a great combination of seasonal ingredients to make a simple and delicious autumnal dish. It does make a difference if you can source some good-quality black pudding: your butcher should be able to help you out here. This is the kind of earthy, country food that I adore.

SERVES 4

4 thick slices best-quality
    black pudding
olive oil
400g smoked eel fillets, cut into
    long angled pieces
watercress or parsley, to garnish

FOR THE CIDER
MUSTARD SAUCE
20g unsalted butter
1 white onion, peeled and
    finely diced
1 garlic clove, peeled and crushed
2 sprigs fresh thyme
100ml cider vinegar
330ml dry cider
250ml chicken stock (see page 222)
200ml double cream
1 tbsp Dijon mustard
1 tbsp wholegrain mustard
salt and pepper

FOR THE CARAMELISED
APPLES
3 Cox's apples, unpeeled but cored
    and quartered (rub them with
    lemon juice to stop oxidation)
100g unsalted butter
150g soft brown sugar
100ml cider vinegar

To make the cider mustard sauce, melt the butter in a saucepan and sweat off the onion with the garlic clove and the thyme. When the onions are translucent add the cider vinegar and cider and reduce until almost gone. Add the chicken stock and reduce by half, then add the cream and bring to the boil. Add the mustards, taste and season. Reserve.

To caramelise the apples, in a warm pan, sauté the apples in the butter for 6–8 minutes, to golden brown. Add the brown sugar and cider vinegar, and cook until the apples are soft and golden in colour. Remove from the heat and reserve.

Over a medium heat, fry the black pudding in some olive oil until crisp on the outside and hot in the middle, for about 3–4 minutes.

Arrange the black pudding on four plates and spoon over the apples. Place 4–5 pieces of eel on top and spoon round the cider mustard sauce. Garnish with some watercress or parsley.

ELDERBERRY, PIGEON AND SNAIL BRUSCHETTA

I get very over-excited about this kind of earthy, gutsy food. It's simply the best the season has to offer, put together in a sympathetic way.

SERVES 2

1 wood pigeon or farmed squab
salt and pepper
50g salted butter
1 splash ruby port
1 heaped tbsp fresh elderberries
1 sprig fresh thyme
1 garlic clove, peeled and crushed
1 shallot, peeled and diced
6 prepared snails (fresh, canned or frozen)
a few shelled cobnuts (or hazelnuts)
a small handful of flat-leaf parsley leaves, roughly chopped

TO SERVE

2 slices stale country-style bread or ciabatta
1 garlic clove, peeled
extra virgin olive oil

Preheat the grill or chargrill, and preheat the oven to 180°C/350°F/ Gas 4.

Spatchcock the bird by removing the backbone and flattening it out (your butcher should do this for you). Season and grill or chargrill for 3–4 minutes on both sides to colour and start the cooking. Put into a roasting tin and roast in the oven for a further 4–5 minutes for rare, depending upon the thickness of the bird. When it is done, there should be a slight spring in the breast and the flesh should be pink all the way through, but not flabby.

Remove the tin from the oven, and throw in half the butter, a slug of port and the elderberries. Allow the bird to rest in the pan to collect any juices; this will be the finished sauce.

In a frying pan, heat half the butter, the thyme, garlic and shallot together. When it starts to foam, chuck in the snails and sauté for a few minutes. Add the cobnuts and toast for a further few minutes to colour. Add the parsley. Remove and reserve.

Finally chargrill the bread on both sides, rub with a raw garlic clove and lightly sprinkle with good olive oil.

Quarter the pigeon, allowing half per person, and place on the bread. Scatter over the snails and cobnuts, and lightly dress with the cooking juices, port and elderberries. Serve.

MARINATED POUSSIN SALAD

Try and find time to marinate the poussin. It takes a bit of forward
planning but ultimately it is a very simple and extremely satisfying dish.

SERVES 2-4 (AS STARTER
OR MAIN)

2 poussin
2 tsp salt
4 tsp brown sugar
3 fresh red chillies, chopped
100g fresh coriander stalks and
   roots, finely chopped
vegetable oil
100g picked fresh coriander leaves
50g picked fresh mint leaves
2 tbsp sesame seeds
about 250g Japanese mooli or
   daikon radish, shredded
4–5 tbsp soy sauce
juice of 2 limes

Spatchcock the bird by removing the backbone and flattening it out
(your butcher should do this for you). Put the poussin in a suitable
dish. Mix the salt, sugar, chillies and coriander stalks and roots
together and marinate the poussin in this for 3–4 days in the fridge.

Preheat the oven to 180°C/350°F/Gas 4.

When ready to cook, pan-fry the poussin in a little oil for a few
minutes to colour, then cook in the preheated oven for 20–25 minutes.
Remove and allow to rest.

Make a salad from the coriander and mint leaves, sesame seeds and
shredded radish. Dress with the soy sauce, lime juice and the meat
juices from the pan.

Portion the poussin. Cut in half lengthways, remove the legs, and
serve 1 or 2 legs and breast per person. Arrange on a plate with the
dressed salad.

POACHED PHEASANT WITH GIN-SOAKED MUSCAT GRAPES

This recipe makes an ideal winter starter or a light main course. It needs some forward planning to marinate the grapes — but you could make a batch and use them in other dishes.

SERVES 2 COMFORTABLY

1 pheasant breast
500ml light game or chicken stock
450g baby spinach
olive oil

FOR THE GIN-SOAKED GRAPES
350ml water
330g caster sugar
1kg black seedless Muscat or other good-quality grapes
1 sprig fresh thyme
1 bay leaf
a few juniper berries
40ml good gin

Boil the water and sugar together to melt the sugar. Remove from the heat and cool. Wash the grapes and put them in a container with the aromatics. Add the gin and enough of the sugar syrup to cover. Store for a few weeks.

Poach the pheasant breast until medium rare in the game or chicken stock for no longer than 6–8 minutes. Do not allow to boil. Reserve.

In a frying pan, cook the baby spinach in some olive oil and some of the poaching liquor for about 1 minute.

Slice the pheasant breast and place on a serving plate alongside some spinach, then spoon the gin-soaked grapes over the pheasant.

PRINGAS WITH SOURDOUGH TOAST

I first tried pringas in southern Spain. It's a lot like a rillette or coarse pâté. It makes a great starter, tapas dish, or a filling snack for any time of day. You can play around with the different meats and sausages you use, but this recipe is fairly close to the original.

SERVES 4–6

FOR THE PRINGAS
200g pork fat or lardo
1 onion, peeled and quartered
3 celery sticks, chopped
2 bay leaves
4 garlic cloves, peeled and
   left whole
a small bunch fresh thyme
a pinch of saffron
1 tsp black peppercorns
200g beef brisket
300g pork belly
200g cooking chorizo, cut into
   large pieces
250g black pudding, cut into
   large pieces
4 chicken thighs
1 piece bone marrow (100–150g),
   cleaned
2 tsp hot smoked paprika
2 tsp sweet smoked paprika
salt and pepper
cornichons or a selection of
   pickles, to serve

FOR THE SOURDOUGH
TOAST
4–6 slices sourdough
3 tbsp olive oil
2 garlic cloves, peeled and
   left whole

To make the pringas, melt half the fat in a casserole or large saucepan over a medium heat. Add the onion quarters, celery, bay leaves, garlic, thyme, saffron and peppercorns and cook until coloured and softened. Add all the meats and the marrow, cover with water and simmer for 3 hours until tender. Remove and shred all of the meat, keeping the vegetables and discarding the bones, bay and thyme stalks. Strain the sauce into the another pan and reduce by half on the hob.

Heat the remaining fat in a large frying pan and cook out the smoked paprikas for about 2 minutes. Add the shredded meat and vegetables to the pan with the reduced sauce, season with salt and pepper and mash everything together well.

Brush the sourdough slices with the oil. Place the bread on a hot griddle and cook on both sides until toasted. Rub both sides with the garlic cloves. Serve with the shredded meat and pickles.

MAINS

GNOCCHI, ONION PURÉE, KALE AND BLACK GARLIC

This is an easy-to-follow gnocchi recipe made very tasty indeed by the addition of onion purée and black garlic paste.

SERVES 4

2 large baking potatoes (around
    600g), scrubbed
80g Parmesan, freshly grated,
    plus 20g to serve
2 free-range egg yolks, beaten
150g Italian 00 plain flour, plus
    extra for dusting
salt and pepper
10g salted butter

FOR THE ONION PURÉE
1 tbsp olive oil
1 white onion, peeled and chopped
8 garlic cloves, peeled and chopped
1 bay leaf

FOR THE BLACK
GARLIC PASTE
10 black garlic cloves, peeled
2 tbsp olive oil
a pinch of salt

FOR THE KALE
200g kale, thick spines discarded
    and leaves chopped
50ml olive oil
juice of 1 lemon

Preheat the oven to 200°C/400°F/Gas 6. Place the potatoes on a baking tray and cook for 1 hour, or until cooked through.

Once cool enough to handle, remove the flesh from the potatoes and push through a fine sieve or ricer into a large bowl. Leave to cool completely and then stir in the Parmesan, yolks and flour. Season with salt and pepper. Bring the mixture together to form a dough. Lightly dust a work surface with flour and roll the dough out into a long sausage shape. With a sharp knife cut the dough into dumpling shapes of about 2cm. Set aside.

For the onion purée, heat the oil in a frying pan and add the onion, garlic and bay leaf. Sweat for a few minutes until the onions are softened but not coloured. Remove the bay leaf and place the onions and garlic in a blender or food processor. Blitz to a purée and pass through a sieve into a small bowl.

For the black garlic paste, blitz the garlic, oil and salt in a blender or food processor to create a paste. Add water if you need more liquid.

Put the kale on a chopping board and massage the leaves with the olive oil, until they soften and break down. Add the lemon juice and season with salt and pepper.

Meanwhile, bring a large saucepan of salted water to the boil and add the gnocchi pieces. Simmer until they rise to the top of the water and then remove with a slotted spoon. Throw them into a hot sauté pan and fry in a little butter until golden all over.

To serve, spoon the onion purée onto warmed plates. Swirl on the black garlic paste and add the gnocchi and kale on top. Scatter with grated Parmesan.

SESAME CAULIFLOWER STEAKS WITH TAHINI CHICKPEAS

I love the versatility of cauliflower. Just remember that, like other veg, quality is often key. Even though they may all look the same, good-quality cauliflowers will have more flavour.

SERVES 2

FOR THE CAULIFLOWER STEAKS
2 tbsp sesame seeds
1 tbsp coriander seeds, crushed
½ tbsp cumin seeds, crushed
1 tsp ground black pepper
½ tsp turmeric
½ tsp smoked paprika
2 tbsp olive oil, plus extra
   for drizzling
1 large cauliflower, cut into 4 steaks
25g unsalted butter, melted
1 lemon, thinly sliced

FOR THE TAHINI DRESSING
1 garlic bulb, halved
salt and pepper
2 tbsp olive oil, plus extra for
   roasting the garlic
50g tahini
juice of 1 lemon

FOR THE TOASTED SMOKY CHICKPEAS
3 tbsp cooked chickpeas
1 tsp smoked paprika
3 tbsp olive oil
a pinch of salt
3 tbsp pomegranate seeds

TO GARNISH
2 tbsp chopped fresh mint
2 tbsp chopped fresh coriander

Preheat the oven to 200°C/400°F/Gas 6.

For the tahini dressing, place the halved garlic bulb with some salt, pepper and olive oil in foil, wrap it up and roast for 45 minutes.

For the cauliflower, place the sesame seeds, crushed coriander and cumin seeds, black pepper, turmeric, smoked paprika and oil into a large bowl and mix. Add the cauliflower and toss to coat. Place the cauliflower steaks in a roasting dish with a drizzle of olive oil, the melted butter and lemon slices. Make sure the steaks are well coated. Roast in the oven for 15–20 minutes.

To finish the tahini dressing, squeeze the roasted garlic cloves out into a bowl. Place the tahini, lemon juice, olive oil and garlic into a food processor and blend until smooth. Add a little hot water to thin the dressing if it is too thick. Add salt to taste.

For the chickpeas, place in a bowl and toss with the paprika, oil and salt. Lay on a baking tray and roast in the oven, alongside the cauliflower, for 20 minutes to crisp. Place in a bowl and toss with the pomegranate seeds.

To serve, spoon the dressing onto plates and place the cauliflower steaks and lemon slices on top. Garnish with the crisp chickpeas and the mint and coriander.

SPRING VEGETABLE RISOTTO

Quite often vegetable-based dishes are labelled 'primavera' all year round, but the whole point of a risotto or pasta 'primavera' is making the most of the very first broad beans, fennel, asparagus, leeks, baby carrots and peas early in the season.

It is a perfect British dish – because we do love our vegetable gardens and this is the perfect way to use the best of the crop. The dominant force should be the fresh vegetables, bound in the creamy rice but not the other way around – it should be a light, colourful dish.

SERVES 4

150g shelled broad beans
150g fresh peas
8–10 small asparagus spears
1.5 litres vegetable stock
a few Parmesan rinds
1 large white onion, peeled
    and diced
olive oil
50g salted butter, plus extra
    to finish
1 garlic clove, finely chopped
a few sprigs fresh thyme, leaves
    picked
250g Carnaroli or Arborio rice
125ml good-quality fruity
    white wine
100g Parmesan, freshly grated
salt and pepper
1 squeeze lemon juice

Firstly, prepare the vegetables. Blanch the beans, peas and asparagus in a saucepan of boiling water, then refresh in iced water. Drain well and keep to one side.

At this point have the vegetable stock boiling away, with the Parmesan rinds thrown in for flavour.

In a large frying pan, sweat off the diced onion in a big splash of olive oil and 25g of the butter. Add the garlic clove and thyme. This should take about 10 minutes of slow cooking – do not colour the onion at all.

Stir the rice into the onions for a few moments. When the rice is begging for liquid, throw in the white wine and the rice will now start sizzling. Keep stirring to evaporate the liquid. Then add the hot stock slowly, ladle by ladle, so that the rice incorporates each spoonful quickly. Stir throughout to prevent the rice from sticking and speed up the evaporation. Continue doing this for 15–20 minutes, until the rice is almost cooked and the stock is almost used up. Now throw in the vegetables, add most of the Parmesan and season.

Add the squeeze of lemon if some acidity is needed. Add the rest of the butter at this stage for extra richness. Stir the risotto and add a touch more stock if required – the consistency should be a little loose at this stage. Allow to rest in the pan for a few minutes to relax and absorb the rest of the liquid. Serve still quite wet with the remaining freshly grated Parmesan.

NOTE
Fresh herbs such as tarragon or chervil could be added at the end of the cooking to lighten the risotto. If the idea of blanching the vegetables bores you, then throw them all in at the beginning of the dish when the onion is added. (The vegetables will lose some colour, but the risotto will still be delicious!)

WARM SALAD OF SPICED AUBERGINE AND RED CABBAGE

This is a delicious little vegetarian dish that will spice up any festive menu.

SERVES 4

¼ red cabbage, shredded
salt
2 aubergines
50g caster sugar
150ml soy sauce
2 garlic cloves, peeled and minced
1 tsp minced fresh ginger
150ml mirin
2 fresh red chillies, sliced
4 spring onions, thinly sliced
vegetable oil, for frying

TO SERVE
1 small bunch chopped coriander
1 tbsp chopped mint
20g toasted and crushed
   cashew nuts

First, season the red cabbage in a colander with some salt and leave to soften while you do everything else.

Slice the aubergines into 1cm-thick rounds. In a bowl, mix the sugar, soy, garlic, ginger, mirin, chillies and spring onions together and set aside.

Heat the vegetable oil in a frying pan over a high heat and shallow fry the aubergine in batches for a few minutes until soft in the middle. Remove and drain on kitchen paper. Keep warm while you repeat the process with the rest of the aubergines.

When all the aubergines are cooked and they are still warm, dress in most of the soy mix. Toss the rest of the dressing through the softened red cabbage.

To serve, layer the aubergines with some of the chopped herbs and the red cabbage. Garnish with the rest of the fresh herbs and the toasted cashew nuts.

SPICED LENTILS WITH CRÈME FRAÎCHE

This is a warming dish eaten on its own from a big bowl with lots of fresh bread, but it is also good as an accompaniment to something like a simple roast chicken.

SERVES 2 AS A MAIN, 4 AS
AN ACCOMPANIMENT

50g olive oil
1 tsp ground coriander
1 tsp ground turmeric
1 tsp ground cumin
1 small knob fresh ginger, grated
2 garlic cloves, peeled and
    left whole
1 fresh red chilli, diced
½ white onion, peeled and
    finely diced
1 celery stick, finely diced
100g chunk smoked bacon
    (optional), diced
200g dried Puy or Umbrian lentils
salt and pepper
100g crème fraîche or soured
    cream, to serve

Heat the oil in a frying pan and fry the ground spices to extract all their flavour.

Toss in the ginger, garlic and chilli. Keep an eye on the pan to ensure the spices do not burn. Throw in the onion and celery, sweat for 5 minutes, and add the bacon, if desired. Then add the lentils and dry fry them in the mix for a few minutes.

Cover with water and simmer for 15–20 minutes until just cooked. The lentils should retain their bite.

Season and serve with a dollop of crème fraîche or soured cream.

ROASTED COD WITH A PRAWN CRUST, LEEKS AND BUTTERY MASH

This is a great way to make cod a bit more interesting, while still creating a homely, tasty dish.

SERVES 2

FOR THE COD
2 slices white bread, crusts removed
100g raw prawns, minced
juice of ½ lemon
2 cod fillets (250g each)
2 tbsp olive oil
lemon wedges, to serve

FOR THE MASH
500g Maris Piper potatoes, peeled
    and roughly chopped
75ml whole milk
75ml double cream
75g salted butter
1 bay leaf
2 garlic cloves, peeled and crushed
½ small bunch fresh thyme
salt and pepper

FOR THE SAUTÉED LEEKS
1 tbsp olive oil
10g salted butter
1 leek, trimmed and finely chopped
1–2 sprigs fresh thyme

Preheat the oven to 220°C/425°F/Gas 7.

Roll the slices of bread thinly using a rolling pin and trim to fit the size of the cod fillets. Mix the prawns and lemon juice together in a bowl. Spread half the prawns on each slice of bread and lay the cod fillets on top. Transfer to the fridge to chill for 30 minutes.

Heat the oil in a frying pan and add the cod, bread-side down. Cook until the bread is lightly golden, then flip over and transfer to a baking tray, cod-side down. Roast for 6–8 minutes, or until the cod is cooked through. Leave to rest.

Meanwhile, to make the buttery mash, place the potatoes in a large saucepan of water over a high heat and bring to the boil. Reduce the heat and simmer for 15 minutes, or until the potatoes are tender. Drain in a colander and leave until all the steam has evaporated. Mash lightly and then push through a fine sieve or potato ricer.

Place the milk, cream, butter, bay leaf, garlic and thyme in a large saucepan over a low heat and simmer gently for 20 minutes. Strain through a sieve and beat the milk into the mashed potatoes. Season with salt and pepper.

To make the sautéed leeks, heat the oil and butter in a small frying pan and add the leek and thyme. Fry for 4–5 minutes until golden brown.

Spoon the mash onto warmed plates, top with the leeks and finish with the cod. Serve with lemon wedges.

ROASTED MONKFISH WITH WILD MUSHROOM BROTH

Meaty monkfish goes brilliantly with pancetta. The rosemary-infused butter makes it a good dinner-party dish. Caul fat can be ordered from your butcher with a bit of notice; it does help keep the dish together. If you fancy, add a few drops of truffle oil at the end.

SERVES 2

FOR THE CONFIT GARLIC
cloves from 2 garlic bulbs, peeled
olive oil
2 sprigs fresh thyme
1 bay leaf

FOR THE ROASTED
MONKFISH
400–450g monkfish fillet
6 blanched leek leaves, dark green
    parts only
6 thin slices pancetta
caul fat, to wrap
25g unsalted butter
1 bay leaf
1 sprig fresh rosemary
1 garlic clove, peeled and smashed

FOR THE WILD
MUSHROOM BROTH
2 shallots, peeled and
    finely chopped
2 garlic cloves, peeled and
    left whole
2 tbsp olive oil
400g wild mushrooms,
    roughly chopped
1 tbsp dried porcini mushrooms,
    soaked in boiling water
25ml Madeira
500ml chicken stock (see page 222)
salt and pepper

TO SERVE
1 bunch watercress
a few drops of truffle oil (optional)

To make the garlic confit, place the garlic cloves in a small saucepan and cover with olive oil. Add the thyme and bay leaf and poach over a medium heat for 1 hour. Allow to cool and then break the garlic with a fork to a rough purée.

Preheat the oven to 200°C/400°F/Gas 6. Wrap the monkfish in the leek leaves, followed by the sliced pancetta. Then spread with the garlic confit and wrap in the caul fat.

Heat an ovenproof pan over a medium heat and add the butter, bay leaf, rosemary and garlic, then add the monkfish. Allow it to colour while basting in the butter. Transfer to the hot oven for 12–14 minutes or until cooked through, then remove from the oven and set aside to rest.

To make the wild mushroom broth, sauté the shallots and garlic in the oil for about 5 minutes until soft, then add the wild mushrooms and rehydrated porcini. Sauté for 4–5 minutes until the mushrooms are golden, then add the Madeira. Cook until the Madeira has reduced by half and then add the stock. Bring to the boil, taste and season with sea salt and freshly ground black pepper.

To serve, slice the monkfish into rounds. Spoon some wild mushrooms into a serving bowl and add some of the broth. Top with the fish and garnish with watercress and truffle oil, if liked.

MUSSEL AND SAFFRON BRANDADE, WITH BACON CRUMBS

Rich, fat mussels, soft melting potato and the crunch of smoked bacon – just a great combination of textures and flavours.

SERVES 4

1kg mussels (shelled weight, 2kg in shell), scrubbed and debearded
350ml white wine
1 bay leaf
2 sprigs fresh thyme
200ml double cream
100ml olive oil
½ garlic bulb, cut in half
a pinch of good saffron strands
700g mashed potato (see page 153)
salt and pepper
4 medium free-range eggs

FOR THE BACON CRUMBS
2 rashers streaky bacon
olive oil
panko or breadcrumbs

Begin by tapping each mussel with a knife, discarding any that do not close. Steam the mussels in a pan in the white wine with the bay leaf and thyme for 3–4 minutes, covered, until the mussels open. Discard any that do not open fully.

Strain and reserve the juices. Remove the mussel meat from the shells when cool. Set aside. Strain the mussel liquor through a sieve or kitchen cloth to remove any grit.

Warm the cream, olive oil and garlic in a saucepan with the saffron, to infuse. Stir the infused cream bit by bit into the warm mashed potato, plus some of the mussel liquor, until you have a soft but not too wet mixture. The consistency should hold its own weight. Taste and season, making sure you have included all the saffron strands.

Stir in the mussel meat. Keep warm.

To make the bacon crumbs, in a frying pan over a high heat fry the bacon in a little oil until crisp. Remove from the pan, then throw in the panko, toss and toast until golden. Blitz the bacon in a food processor with the panko. Reserve while you soft poach the eggs.

Serve the mussel brandade with a poached egg per person and some toasted bacon crumbs.

MIXED SEAFOOD STEW WITH SPICY MAYONNAISE

We served this at Alastair Little's restaurant every day for over two years. It is still one of my most enjoyable dishes to prepare and serve. This is a great one for putting in the middle of the table and letting everyone dig in. It is fine to use a selection of seafood or just one fish.

SERVES 4

about 800g fish: say 100g thick
    white fish fillet per person,
    2 scallops each, a handful of
    mussels and/or clams and
    80g brown shrimps
seasoned plain flour
olive oil
croutons, to serve

FOR THE FISH STOCK
olive oil
2 celery sticks, sliced
2 carrots, diced
1 white onion, peeled and diced
1 garlic bulb, smashed up
1 star anise
1 fresh red chilli
1 small bunch fresh thyme
a few fresh tarragon stalks
bay leaves
about 2kg fish trimmings from
    good white fish (no eyes, gills or
    oily fish; crab, lobster and prawn
    shells are really good), all rinsed
1 tbsp tomato purée
125ml Noilly Prat

FOR THE SPICY MAYONNAISE
1 dried red chilli, crushed
4 garlic cloves, peeled
1 roasted and peeled red pepper,
    from a jar
2 tsp hot smoked paprika
a small pinch of saffron strands
1 recipe basic mayonnaise, about
    300ml (see tartare sauce on
    page 230)
juice of 1 lemon, or to taste

If using shellfish, tap each shell with a knife, discarding any that do not close.

Heat a film of oil in a large frying pan and throw in the celery, carrots and onion. Sweat for 10 minutes or so. Add the aromatics and stir in the fish bits. Continue stirring erratically for 5–10 minutes.

Add the tomato purée and cook out for a further 2 minutes, then throw in the Noilly Prat. Boil the alcohol for a few minutes. Cover the fish pieces with water and simmer for 45 minutes, stirring occasionally to avoid the fish bones sticking to the bottom of the pan. Pour through a colander and skim off any of that orangey-looking fat.

For the spicy mayonnaise, mash in a pestle and mortar, or blitz together in a blender, the chilli, garlic, pepper, paprika and saffron. Then stir through the mayonnaise in a bowl and add lemon juice to taste. Rest to allow the flavours to develop.

Now lightly dust the fish fillets or chunks in some seasoned flour and fry them off in a little hot oil for 3–4 minutes until golden. Turn them over and then add the scallops. When you have colour on these, turn them over and add a ladle of the stock and the mussels and/or clams. Gently simmer to finish the cooking. Add the brown shrimps and stir through for a couple of minutes. Do not let the stock boil as the shellfish will toughen.

Push the fish to one side and introduce a large spoonful of spicy mayonnaise. Gently shimmy the pan around to incorporate the mayonnaise and allow the soup to thicken.

Serve immediately with croutons and some more of the mayonnaise.

CRAB AND SAMPHIRE FRITTATA WITH BROWN CRAB DRESSING

The trick with this recipe is to leave the middle just slightly runny. Over-cooking, just like with an omelette, kills the dish.

SERVES 2

100g fresh brown crab meat
1 tbsp crème fraîche
salt and pepper
lemon juice
whole milk, to thin the sauce
40g freshly picked marsh or
    rock samphire
100g fresh white crab meat
100g each chopped fresh chervil,
    dill and chives
6 medium free-range eggs
olive oil

Preheat the grill to the highest temperature.

Put the brown crab meat in a mixer and add the crème fraîche, some salt and pepper and a squeeze of lemon juice. Sieve the sauce and let it down with some milk until you have a sauce-like consistency. Reserve.

Blanch the samphire in a saucepan of boiling water. Remove and refresh in cold water. Reserve. Mix the white crab meat with the fresh herbs and some salt, pepper and lemon juice.

To make the frittata, beat the eggs lightly in a bowl and season. Drop into a small warm, lightly oiled pan. Pull the eggs away from the side. Put the white crab meat mix in the middle. Top with the samphire and shuffle the mix about to mingle with the egg. Finish under the hot grill to 'soufflé' a little and cook the eggs.

Serve on a big white plate with the brown crab meat dressing around.

CURRIED SEA BASS CHOWDER

This tasty fish dish is very easy to knock together – with great results!

SERVES 2

FOR THE CHOWDER
50g unsalted butter
1 potato, peeled and diced
1 leek, diced
2 celery sticks, diced
½ fennel bulb, diced
2 garlic cloves, peeled and
   finely chopped
1 tbsp mild curry powder
1 star anise
50ml white vermouth
500ml fish stock (see page 220)
100–150ml crème fraîche
salt and pepper
6 spring onions, diced, to garnish

FOR THE SEA BASS
2 sea bass fillets, skin removed
   (250g each)
2 tbsp olive oil
bunch finely snipped fresh chives

To make the chowder, heat the butter in a frying pan and gently fry the potato, leek, celery, fennel and garlic over a medium–low heat for 10 minutes. Add the curry powder and star anise. Pour in the vermouth and cook until reduced by half. Pour in the fish stock. Bring to a simmer and cook for 10 minutes, until the potato is cooked through. Stir in the crème fraîche and season with salt and pepper.

To cook the sea bass, brush the skin with the oil and press the chives evenly all over the fish. Lay the fillets on top of the simmering chowder and poach gently for 5 minutes until cooked through.

Serve the chowder in bowls with a sea bass fillet on top and garnish with the spring onions.

WILD SEA BASS, SMOKED PAPRIKA AND BRAISED WHITE BEANS

Piquillo peppers, rocket and smoked paprika make a spicy accompaniment to these crisp fillets of sea bass.

SERVES 2

best-quality extra virgin olive oil
2 wild sea bass fillets, trimmed
   and skin scored
knob of salted butter
juice of 1 lemon
salt and pepper

FOR THE BEANS

250g dried cannellini beans, soaked
   in cold water overnight
1 sprig rosemary
1 fresh red chilli
2 bay leaves
1 onion, peeled and quartered
1 carrot, peeled
1 celery stick
a pinch of smoked paprika
100g piquillo peppers, diced
a handful of rocket leaves
juice of ½ lemon
olive oil

Drain the soaked beans and transfer to a large saucepan. Add the rosemary, red chilli, bay leaves, onion, carrot and celery. Pour over enough water to cover by 3cm. Bring to the boil and simmer for approximately 1½ hours or until the beans are soft. You will need to top up the water from time to time.

When the beans are cooked, remove from the heat and drain in a colander, reserving the cooking liquor. Lift out the vegetables, herbs and red chilli. Chop up the chilli and add back into the beans along with the smoked paprika and enough of the cooking liquor to give the beans a loose consistency. Stir through the piquillo peppers, rocket, lemon juice and a drizzle of olive oil.

For the sea bass, preheat a frying pan over a medium heat and add a little olive oil. Season the bass skin and fry the fillets skin-side down for 4–5 minutes until crisp. Turn the fillets over, add the butter and a squeeze of lemon and cook for a further minute.

To serve, place a spoonful of the beans on a plate and top it with the bass. Squeeze over the remaining lemon juice and drizzle with extra virgin olive oil.

MUSSELS COOKED IN BEER WITH CRISPY MONKFISH CHEEKS

If you can't get hold of monkfish cheeks, then chunky slices of monkfish tail will also work. It's fun to experiment with different types of beer – I've used a wheat one here.

SERVES 4

FOR THE MONKFISH CHEEKS
200g plain flour, plus 1 tbsp
    for dusting
2 tsp fresh yeast
200ml wheat beer
125ml sparkling water
3 monkfish cheeks, cut into
    3cm pieces

FOR THE MUSSELS
1kg mussels, scrubbed and
    debearded
2 tbsp vegetable oil
1 banana shallot, peeled and
    finely chopped
1 tsp coriander seeds
1 lemongrass stick, finely chopped
2 lime leaves
500ml wheat beer
100ml double cream
1 tbsp chopped parsley
1 tbsp chopped dill
salt and pepper
juice of 1 lime

For the deep-fried monkfish cheeks, in a bowl whisk the 200g flour, the yeast, beer and sparkling water in a bowl until you have a loose batter. Leave to stand for 30 minutes until foaming.

Meanwhile, if any mussels are open, tap them lightly on a hard surface. If they don't close, discard them.

Heat the oil in a frying pan (that has a lid) and sauté the shallots, coriander seeds, lemongrass and lime leaves until softened. Add the mussels and pour in the beer. Put the lid on and steam for 5 minutes until the mussels have opened. (Discard any that remain closed.) Pick the mussel meat from the shells and return to the broth. Reduce until the volume of the liquid has reduced by half.

Pour in the cream and add most of the chopped herbs. Season with salt and pepper and squeeze over the lime. Keep warm.

Preheat a deep-fat fryer to 180°C/350°F.

Coat the monkfish pieces in the extra flour and then dip into the batter. Carefully lower into the oil and deep-fry for 5–6 minutes until golden. Drain on kitchen paper.

Serve the deep-fried monkfish cheeks on top of the mussels and garnish with the remaining herbs.

SMOKED SALMON PIZZA

Once you get the hang of these thin crisp-based pizzas, you can experiment with all sorts of toppings. They are intentionally thin so that the focus is on the flavours and textures on top, not on a thick, doughy base. The dough here freezes well in balls to be cooked at a later date.

MAKES 2 LARGE PIZZAS, TO SERVE 2-4

FOR THE PIZZA DOUGH
900g Italian 00 plain flour, plus extra for dusting
550ml water
25g fresh yeast
15g salt

FOR THE PIZZA TOPPING
500g San Marzano tomatoes, finely diced
20g fresh oregano leaves
salt and pepper
extra virgin olive oil
4 tbsp soured cream
150–300g smoked salmon
10g fresh thyme or dill sprigs, or a herb of your choice, to garnish

To make the pizza dough, mix 550g of the flour, the water and fresh yeast together in a bowl to make a sponge. Cover with clingfilm and leave to rise for 1 hour.

Add the remaining flour and the salt, then mix and knead well. Roll into two balls, and allow to rise on a lightly floured tray in the fridge for half an hour. If you want to make smaller pizzas, you can: any remaining dough will freeze well.

Preheat the oven to its highest possible heat.

Roll out each pizza base until quite thin. Scatter over the diced tomatoes and oregano, season lightly and drizzle over the olive oil. Bake in the preheated oven until the dough is risen and slightly charred on the edges.

Remove, dot with the soured cream and lay the salmon over. Flash back through the oven for 30 seconds to take the chill off the salmon. Remove and scatter over your preferred herb. Serve immediately.

GRILLED SALMON SALAD WITH TARRAGON SAUCE

This simple salmon recipe is elevated to new heights and given some punch by a traditional Italian tarragon dressing. The dressing also works well with cold roasted beef or a piece of grilled chicken.

SERVES 2

FOR THE SAUCE

1 slice day-old bread,
  crusts removed
50–75ml red wine vinegar
1 hard-boiled free-range
  egg yolk, grated
2 anchovy fillets, finely chopped
1 tbsp baby capers, finely chopped
1 garlic clove, peeled and minced
1 tbsp finely chopped fresh tarragon
2 tbsp olive oil
salt and pepper

FOR THE SALMON

2 organic or good-quality salmon
  fillets, skin on (200g each)
salt and ground white pepper
juice of 1 lemon

FOR THE SALAD

100g smoked pancetta, cubed
4 tbsp fresh tarragon leaves
4 tbsp frisée leaves
1 banana shallot, peeled and
  finely chopped
50g lamb's lettuce
1 tsp red wine vinegar
2 tbsp olive oil

To make the sauce, place the bread in a bowl and pour over the vinegar. Leave to soften while you mix the other ingredients, except the olive oil, in a large bowl. Squeeze the excess vinegar from the bread and finely chop, then add to the bowl along with enough oil to make a loose consistency. Season with salt and pepper and set aside.

Season the salmon with salt and white pepper. Heat a griddle pan until hot, then cook the salmon on both sides for about 8 minutes, until cooked through but still a little pink. Squeeze over some lemon juice and leave to rest.

To make the salad, place the pancetta in a small frying pan over a medium heat and fry until crisp. Reserve the oil for the dressing and drain the pancetta on kitchen paper.

Toss the tarragon, frisée leaves, shallot and lamb's lettuce together in a large salad bowl, then sprinkle over the pancetta. Mix the pancetta cooking oil from the frying pan with the red wine vinegar and olive oil and use this to lightly dress the salad. Season with salt and pepper.

To serve, spoon the sauce onto a serving plate, add the salad and then flake over the salmon.

WILD SALMON, SAMPHIRE AND CRAYFISH SAUCE

I like to put together ingredients that have a natural affinity, so salmon and crayfish together on a plate makes sense to me. I also like to use crayfish whenever I can to do my bit to reduce the effects of their invasion of British rivers.

SERVES 4

FOR THE CRAYFISH SAUCE
1kg live crayfish
1 white onion, peeled and diced
1 garlic clove, peeled and cut in half
2 sprigs fresh tarragon
15g fresh thyme leaves
1 tbsp fennel seeds
2 bay leaves
50g unsalted butter
125ml Martini or Noilly Prat
1 litre fresh fish stock (see
    page 220)
250ml double cream
a pinch of smoked paprika
juice of 1 lemon

FOR THE SALMON
4 fillets wild salmon, skin on,
    about 175–225g each
sea salt and pepper
olive oil
about 100g fresh marsh or rock
    samphire, picked over but raw

Kill the crayfish by dropping them into a saucepan of boiling water for 2 minutes. Remove and refresh in cold water. Separate the body from the head and remove the tail meat. Set the meat aside and keep all the shells.

To make the sauce, sweat off the onion and aromatics in half the butter for about 10 minutes, until soft. Add the alcohol when the onions are translucent, and boil to reduce by half. Throw in the crayfish heads, claws and tail shells. Crunch up and stir to extract maximum flavour. Cover with the fish stock and simmer for 20 minutes or until reduced by half. Add the double cream, bring to the boil and season with salt, the paprika and lemon juice. Strain and reserve.

To cook the salmon, score the skin three times on each fillet to prevent curling in the pan. Season the skin side with sea salt. Warm a pan, put in a splash of oil, and pan-fry three-quarters of the way on the skin side, turn over and continue to cook until slightly pink in the middle (5–6 minutes depending on thickness). Remove and keep warm.

Wipe out the pan and throw in the samphire with the remaining butter. Season lightly and sauté for 3 minutes or so until cooked. Throw in the crayfish tails and sauté off for another minute.

To serve, pile up the samphire and crayfish tails, put the wild salmon on top, and spoon around the warmed crayfish sauce.

NOTE
For larger gatherings put a whole side of salmon (ours weighed 1.25kg) on a sheet of non-stick baking paper set on a piece of foil, sprinkle with some chopped tarragon, a little chopped onion, a few fennel seeds, a few sprigs of fresh thyme and salt and black pepper. Dot with butter, add 1 lemon cut into wedges, and a splash of Noilly Prat. Bake uncovered at 200°C/400°F/Gas 6 for about 30 minutes. To check, press the centre of the salmon with a knife. The flakes should be an even colour all the way through; if not, cook for a few more minutes and then re-test.

Photographed overleaf

TUNA WITH RUNNER BEANS, PINE NUTS AND RAISINS

Don't be scared of serving the tuna a little rare. This salad is best served at room temperature or just warm.

SERVES 2

10 blanched almonds
1 bunch each of fresh parsley, mint
  and marjoram (or oregano),
  chopped
2 tuna steaks, about 230g each
50ml freshly squeezed orange juice
1 tsp lemon juice
100ml dry white wine
20g raisins, soaked in hot water
  then drained
30g pine nuts, toasted
200g runner beans, blanched
  and finely sliced

Using a food processor, make a paste with the almonds and herbs.

In a hot, non-stick frying pan, sear the tuna on both sides for 1–2 minutes. Remove from the pan and keep warm.

Deglaze the tuna pan with the citrus juices and white wine, and reduce by half. Add the herb paste, followed by the raisins and pine nuts. Stir in the runner beans and heat through for a few moments.

Throw a pile of the bean salad onto two plates and slice the tuna thickly over the top.

GRILLED SQUID, MERGUEZ SAUSAGE AND COUSCOUS

This dish has got North African overtones. The spicy merguez sausage contains oils which, when cooked, mix beautifully with the squid and couscous.

SERVES 2

50ml extra virgin olive oil
2 merguez sausages
250g fresh squid, cleaned, the
 bodies opened flat (score them
 for a more decorative result)
2 pinches of hot smoked paprika

FOR THE COUSCOUS

150g couscous
sea salt and pepper
finely grated zest of 1 unwaxed
 lemon
½ bunch fresh coriander, chopped
a handful of flat-leaf parsley
 leaves, chopped
1 fresh red chilli, chopped
1 banana shallot, peeled and
 finely sliced
100ml red wine vinegar
a few tbsp of caster sugar

Preheat the oven to 180°C/350°F/Gas 4 and preheat the grill or chargrill.

Put the couscous in a bowl and barely cover with boiling water. Cover the bowl and leave somewhere warm for 10 minutes. Fork through the couscous and add some salt and pepper, the lemon zest, fresh herbs, chilli and shallot. In a small pan heat the red wine vinegar and sugar together until sweet and sour. Add this to the couscous as well and stir through.

Put half the oil in a small roasting tin, add the sausages, and cook for 5 minutes or so in the preheated oven. Let rest to collect some of the oils that come off.

Over a high heat, griddle the squid with a sprinkling of sea salt until it starts to lift off the grill. Remove, drizzle over the remaining olive oil, and leave to rest with the sausages.

To assemble, slice the sausages and jumble with the squid. On each plate, pile up the couscous, top with the squid and sausage, drizzle with some of the cooking oils from the sausage, and throw a pinch of smoked paprika at the dish. Finished.

QUAILS ROASTED IN VINE LEAVES WITH BRANDY

This is a recipe from my old forager friend Raoul's family cookbook, one of many great dishes he shared with me over the years.

SERVES 4

8 quails
salt and pepper
8 vine leaves (a 225g vacuum pack)
olive oil
50ml brandy
450ml chicken stock (see page 222)
4 slices fried bread, halved

Preheat the oven to 180°C/350°F/Gas 4.

Season each quail, wrap in a vine leaf, drizzle with a little olive oil and put in a roasting tin. Roast in the preheated oven for about 10 minutes. Remove from the oven and set the quails aside.

Deglaze the tin with the brandy and flame to remove the alcohol. Add the chicken stock to the tin and put the quails back in, opening out the vine leaves so the breasts can brown. Return to the oven and roast for a further 10 minutes. Remove from the oven and allow to rest a little, catching any juices in the pan.

Top each piece of fried bread with a roasted quail. Serve with the meat juices.

POT-ROAST PHEASANT WITH SMOKED BACON AND CREAM

If you are wary of cooking pheasant, this is a good way to retain moisture in the meat. This dish is very satisfying on a cold evening served with a selection of roasted winter vegetables.

SERVES 2

50g salted butter
1 pheasant
salt and pepper
1 white onion, peeled and cut
    into 1cm dice
2 celery sticks, cut into 1cm dice
1 garlic bulb, cut in half
50g smoked bacon, diced
200ml white wine
2 bay leaves
200ml double cream
a few sprigs fresh thyme

Preheat the oven to 200°C/400°F/Gas 6.

Heat the butter in a casserole. Season the bird, seal in the butter on both sides and remove from the pan. Set aside.

Throw the onion, celery, garlic and smoked bacon into the casserole and sweat for about 10 minutes. Stir in the wine without reducing, then add the bay leaves, cream and thyme and bring up to the boil. Add the pheasant. Place the casserole, uncovered, in the preheated oven for 15 minutes or until cooked. Remove and leave to rest for 10 minutes.

Joint the pheasant, then warm through in the sauce and serve with roasted winter vegetables.

ROAST RABBIT, TOMATOES, OLIVES AND MUSTARD SEEDS

This is a perfect dinner for two. Rabbit is a lean and inexpensive meat and the aromatic sauce makes it something special.

SERVES 2

6–8 wafer-thin slices Bayonne ham
1 bunch fresh basil, leaves only,
    plus a handful of basil leaves,
    tied up, and extra leaves
    to garnish
1 rabbit saddle, bone removed,
    loins separated
50ml olive oil, plus extra for frying
2 garlic cloves, peeled and sliced
1 tbsp mustard seeds
1 shallot, peeled and finely chopped
2 beef tomatoes, finely chopped
1 carrot, peeled
2 tbsp chopped black olives

Lay the ham out on clingfilm and cover with the basil leaves. Lay the rabbit loins on top, overlapping as you go. Top with the saddle and gently roll up into a sausage shape. Tie the clingfilm tightly at both ends. Wrap in a double layer of kitchen foil and chill for 2–3 hours.

Heat the oil in a sauté pan over a medium heat. Add the garlic and mustard seeds and cook until the seeds start to pop. Add the shallot and tomatoes and stir well. Add the whole carrot and the basil bundle and simmer for 10 minutes. Remove the carrot and basil, stir in the olives and set aside.

Preheat the oven to 220°C/425°F/Gas 7.

Remove the foil and clingfilm from the rabbit. Heat a dash of oil in an ovenproof frying pan and add the rabbit. Cook for 2 minutes, turning often, until lightly coloured all over. Transfer to the oven and roast for 6–8 minutes, or until cooked through.

Allow the rabbit to rest for 5 minutes before slicing. Spoon a small amount of the tomato mixture on serving plates and top with slices of rabbit. Garnish with the extra basil leaves and serve.

ROAST DUCK WITH APPLE AND ROSEMARY

The key to really great crispy duck skin is to lose some of the surplus fat just under the skin and then dry out the duck really well. The skin should become like parchment and the flesh beneath stays beautifully moist. Serve with the red cabbage on page 154.

SERVES 2-4

1 large duck
salt and pepper
1 large Bramley apple
1 twig bay leaves
2–3 sprigs fresh rosemary
olive oil

Prick the duck all over to just under the skin. Plunge the whole duck into boiling water, leave for a few minutes, then carefully remove from the pot. Leave to dry in a cool place (in front of an open window or an electric fan is ideal) for a few hours.

Preheat the oven to 220°C/425°F/Gas 7.

When the duck is very dry, season the cavity, then insert the apple and finally the herbs. Season the bird all over and rub lightly with some olive oil. Put it into the preheated oven for 15 minutes to blast the skin into crisping up.

Turn the oven down and cook at 180°C/350°F/Gas 4 for another 40 minutes. Check the bird and baste with the duck fat and apple juices. It may need a little longer, depending on the size of the bird; if so put it back in for another 10–15 minutes and check again. Allow the bird to rest fully for 20 minutes, catching any juices that run out.

These deliciously fatty, flavoursome juices will be your gravy. This is an incredibly rich dish and requires nothing more than simple roast potatoes and red cabbage or maybe a mustard-dressed green salad.

DUCK, ONION AND THYME RISOTTO

This dish is great as it is, but it would be even better with the addition of other duck pieces – like livers, hearts or confit leg meat.

SERVES 4

2 large duck breasts
1.5 litres chicken stock (see page 222)
2 white onions, peeled and finely diced
75g unsalted butter
salt and pepper
1 tbsp fresh thyme leaves
1 garlic clove, peeled and finely crushed
250g Carnaroli or Arborio rice
150ml white wine
50g Parmesan, freshly grated
1 large tbsp mascarpone cheese

Preheat the oven to 180°C/350°F/Gas 4.

Cook the duck breasts to your personal taste, but preferably pink: gently fry in a pan, skin-side down, for 5–6 minutes until golden, then roast in the preheated oven for a further 10–12 minutes. Allow to rest in a warm place and catch the juices that run from the meat.

Meanwhile, for the risotto, have the stock heating through in a saucepan.

In a wide pan, over a medium heat, fry the diced onion in most of the butter with a pinch of salt for about 10 minutes, until soft, then add the thyme leaves and garlic. Stir in the rice and shuffle around the pan for a few minutes until the rice cries out for liquid. Add the white wine and sizzle to reduce. When nearly disappeared, add a ladle of hot stock and continue to do so, stirring, until the stock has all gone and the rice is cooked 'to the bite'. This will take 20 minutes or so.

Finish off the risotto by stirring in the remaining butter, the Parmesan and mascarpone cheese until everything is incorporated. Season.

Now slice the well-rested duck. Arrange over generous spoonfuls of the risotto on individual hot plates, making sure any meat juices are poured over the dish before serving.

GRILLED TURKEY SALAD WITH SPICED PEANUT DRESSING

Yes, you could just use chicken... but I like the overall American feel of all the ingredients in this healthy salad.

SERVES 2

FOR THE GRILLED
TURKEY SALAD
1 small turkey breast, skin off,
    or 2 turkey steaks
2 tbsp olive oil
1 tsp smoked paprika
1 tsp ground cumin
1 tsp ground coriander
1 ripe avocado, halved, de-stoned
    and chopped
3 tbsp natural yoghurt
zest and juice of 2 limes
3 garlic cloves, peeled and minced
salt and pepper

FOR THE SPICED
PEANUT DRESSING
150g peanuts
3 garlic cloves, peeled and chopped
1 banana shallot, peeled
    and chopped
3 dried ancho chillies, rehydrated
    in boiling water

FOR THE GARNISH
1 baby gem lettuce, cut into 4
    and chargrilled
1 bunch coriander, leaves picked
¼ small white cabbage, shredded
    and salted in a colander for
    20 minutes
1 ripe mango, peeled and cut
    into slices.
2 tbsp olive oil
juice of 1 lime

To make the grilled turkey salad, cut the breast into thin steaks and marinate in the olive oil, paprika, cumin and coriander for a few hours. Heat a large griddle pan and chargrill the turkey, cooking on both sides for a few minutes. Remove from the heat and allow to rest before slicing into strips.

In a blender, blitz the avocado, yoghurt, lime and garlic cloves together, taste and season with salt and pepper.

For the spiced peanut dressing, toast the peanuts, garlic and shallots in a hot dry frying pan. Tip into a blender (saving a few tablespoons of the peanuts for the garnish) along with the drained chillies and blitz with enough boiling water (50–100ml) to make a pourable sauce.

To serve, spoon the avocado mixture onto a serving plate and top with a drizzle of the peanut dressing.

Toss all the garnish ingredients lightly in the olive oil and lime juice and scatter on top of the avocado and peanut dressing.

Add the turkey and spoon over more of the peanut dressing, then sprinkle with the reserved chopped peanuts.

SPICED TURKEY BROTH WITH FRAGRANT DUMPLINGS

I find that by Boxing Day I am really looking for something a bit spicy, ideally with lots of chilli. This fits the bill and also fills you up nicely.

SERVES 4

FOR THE BROTH
1 onion, peeled and sliced
3 garlic cloves, peeled and minced
1 leek, sliced
3 celery sticks, sliced
olive oil
a few fresh tarragon sprigs
1 tbsp chopped fresh thyme
1 tbsp 'nduja paste (optional)
125ml white wine
500ml turkey or chicken stock
1 head of cavolo nero, leaves
    stripped from the stems

DUMPLING RECIPE (PAGE 139) WITH THE FOLLOWING ADDED TO THE MIX
zest of 1 unwaxed lemon
a handful of chopped basil leaves
a pinch of chilli flakes

Preheat the oven to 180°C/350°F/Gas 4.

In a casserole dish, sweat the onion, garlic, leek and celery in some olive oil for 10 minutes until soft. Add the tarragon sprigs, chopped thyme and 'nduja paste, if using. Pour in the wine and boil off the alcohol for a few minutes before adding the stock. Simmer gently for another 10 minutes.

Meanwhile make the dumplings as per the recipe on page 139, adding the extra ingredients with the breadcrumbs. Don't roll them too tightly to keep them light. Drop the dumplings into the hot stock, add the torn cavolo nero and put the casserole dish (no lid) in the oven for around 25 minutes. Serve immediately.

ROAST PARTRIDGE WITH FIG, CELERY LEAF AND GORGONZOLA

I like to pair game birds with fruit. It tends to lighten the load. Partridge is quite a delicate bird, and could therefore be a good introduction to game for the novice game-eater.

SERVES 4

4 partridges
4 bay leaves
4 sprigs fresh rosemary
8–12 garlic cloves, peeled
salt and pepper
150g salted butter
8–12 rashers streaky bacon
1 splash red port

FOR THE SALAD
1 head of celery, leaves removed,
    tender inner stalks reserved
20g Gorgonzola cheese, at room
    temperature
4 large black figs
4–5 freshly cracked new-season
    walnuts
1 tbsp olive oil
1 tsp fresh thyme leaves
1 garlic clove, peeled and crushed

FOR THE VINAIGRETTE
200ml olive oil
50ml sherry vinegar or
    red wine vinegar

Preheat the oven to 200°C/400°F/Gas 4.

Stuff the birds with the bay leaves, rosemary and garlic, and season. Add the butter to an ovenproof frying pan over a medium heat and seal off the birds in the foaming butter to colour all over. Cover the breasts with the bacon and roast in the preheated oven for 10–15 minutes until pink. Remove from the oven. Throw the port into the pan and allow to rest for 10 minutes.

Meanwhile, make the salad. Pick the young yellowish celery leaves from the inside and chop the tenderest of the stalks at an angle. Roughly chop the leaves. Crumble the cheese, and quarter the figs.

In a frying pan, over a medium heat, toast the walnuts in the olive oil, with some salt and pepper, the thyme and garlic for a few minutes. Allow to cool and then roughly chop.

Make the vinaigrette by simply mixing the olive oil and vinegar together to emulsify.

To assemble the salad, toss the celery with the walnuts and dress with the vinaigrette. Scatter over the crumbled cheese and quartered figs.

Serve the birds all together on a large plate with a few finger bowls scattered about, with four individual salads. Any remaining vinaigrette can be mixed with the cooking juices and lightly drizzled over the partridges.

ROAST GOOSE

I much prefer a goose for Christmas lunch if we haven't got so many mouths to feed – it doesn't stretch as far as a turkey but there's a lot more flavour and richness to the meat. At other times of the year I like to serve this with baked apples, as they help cut through that richness.

SERVES 6-8

1 goose, 4.5–5kg
salt and pepper
2 bay leaves
1 onion, peeled and cut
    into quarters
2 garlic bulbs, cut through
    the middle
3 tbsp runny honey
2 tbsp chopped fresh thyme

Preheat the oven to 220°C/425°F/Gas 7.

Remove all the excess fat from inside the goose, reserving it for roasting another day. Using a fork, prick the bird all over, especially in the fattest areas. Season the bird all over, and inside. Put the bay leaves, onion and garlic inside.

Brush the bird with the honey and sprinkle over all the thyme. Roast for 30 minutes in the preheated oven before turning down to 170°C/375°F/Gas 3–4 and continue to cook for 1½ hours, draining off and reserving the fat from time to time – there will be a lot! The fat can be used over the next few months to roast potatoes and other such things.

Allow the goose to rest somewhere warm for up to an hour before carving. Serve with all the festive trimmings.

SPEEDY GOOSE CASSOULET

There's never usually much left from a roast goose in our house, but if
do find yourself with some, this is a really quick recipe for knocking up
a tasty cassoulet. You can, of course, use the more traditional duck in
this recipe. Serve with a vinaigrette-dressed green salad.

SERVES 4

200g piece of smoked streaky
    bacon, diced
1 onion, peeled and diced
1 bay leaf
3 celery sticks, diced
2 tbsp goose fat
3 garlic cloves, peeled and minced
1 tbsp chopped fresh thyme
3 good-quality garlic or
    Toulouse sausages
2 x 400g tins cannellini beans
300ml chicken stock (see page 222)
    or leftover goose gravy
around 300g leftover goose meat,
    cut into pieces
50g dried breadcrumbs
50g melted salted butter

Preheat the oven to 180°C/350°F/Gas 4.

In a large frying pan, start by sweating off the diced bacon with the
onion, bay and celery in the goose fat. After 10–15 minutes, add the
garlic and the chopped thyme. Add the whole sausages and brown
them off all over before adding the drained beans.

Tip all this into an ovenproof dish before adding enough of the stock
to loosen but not drown the mix, and then stir in the goose leftovers.
Liberally sprinkle over the breadcrumbs, spoon over the butter and
bake in the oven for 25–30 minutes.

ROAST WOODCOCK

Woodcock is one of the most-prized game birds. They are notoriously difficult to shoot, because of their perfectly camouflaged feathers and their style of flight, twisting and swerving over and around trees and hedges. Woodcock have the most beautifully flavoured flesh and, I think, should be handled with great respect and served in the traditional manner, and – very importantly – only eaten in season.

PER PERSON

1 woodcock, guts left in the bird, trussed in the traditional way with the beak, legs and body tied together
1 bay leaf
1 sprig fresh thyme
2 garlic cloves, peeled
salt and pepper
a little olive oil
25g salted butter
a few strips of salted pork fat, lardo or streaky bacon rashers
1 splash port or Madeira
1 slice stale farmhouse loaf, cut on the angle

Preheat the oven to 200–220°C/400–425°F/Gas 6–7.

Check the birds over for any stray feathers or loose shot. Stuff the herbs and 1 garlic clove in the cavity (still possible to do, despite the guts being inside) and spear the bird with its own beak. Season with salt and pepper.

In a hot pan seal the bird all over in a little olive oil, ensuring a good golden colour on the breasts. When done, smear the butter over the bird, lay the pork fat or bacon over it and put into a roasting tin.

Roast for 10–12 minutes in the preheated hot oven for pink flesh – the only way to eat woodcock. Remove and place the tin on the hob. Deglaze the pan (with the bird still in it) using a splash of the booze, then allow the bird to rest for 5 minutes.

Preheat the grill and toast the bread (or deep-fry for a more traditional result). Rub the toast with the remaining raw garlic clove.

Now the good bit: tip the bird up, beak upwards, and with a spoon remove the guts from the bird. Spread these on the toast, mashing them a little to ensure even cooking, and put under a hot grill for a few minutes to cook.

When done, sit the bird on the toast and tip the resting juices over. Serve with a big bowl of buttered kale or black cabbage and some starch – either mustard celeriac mash or roasted potatoes.

NOTE
For the more adventurous, take a sharp knife and slice the head and beak in half lengthways, exposing the brain. This is what the real foodies want to see and eat (in fact the idea is to use the beak to eat the brain), but this is not one for the faint-hearted.

CHICKEN LIVER TAGLIATELLE WITH CRISPY ONIONS

Something a bit different from the day-to-day pasta dishes we are used to, and it's super-tasty to boot.

SERVES 4

FOR THE BRAISED ONIONS
75g unsalted butter
1 onion, peeled and thinly sliced
2 sprigs fresh thyme, leaves picked
50ml red wine vinegar
50ml balsamic vinegar

FOR THE CHICKEN LIVER TAGLIATELLE
300g tagliatelle
50g unsalted butter
400g chicken livers, cleaned, trimmed and cut in half
2 tbsp balsamic vinegar
200ml chicken stock (see page 222)

TO SERVE
50g crispy onions
2 garlic cloves, peeled and finely chopped
2 tbsp parsley, chopped
4 tbsp Parmesan, freshly grated

To make the braised onions, place a medium sauté pan over a medium heat and add the butter. Once melted, lower the heat and add the onion and thyme. Cook with the lid on for 30–40 minutes or until the onions are soft with no colour. Then stir in the vinegars and cook for a further 5 minutes. Set aside.

Meanwhile, cook the pasta according to the packet instructions.

To cook the chicken livers, heat another medium pan over a medium heat and add the butter. Once hot and melted, add the chicken livers and sauté for 2–3 minutes, or until browned and just cooked through in the middle. Remove from the pan and set aside. Deglaze the pan with the vinegar and then add the braised onions and the stock and cook until the liquid has reduced by half.

When the tagliatelle is cooked, drain and add it to the reduced sauce with the chicken livers. Toss until coated.

Place the crispy onions, garlic, parsley and Parmesan into a small bowl and mix.

To serve, place the hot pasta in serving bowls and top with the crispy onion mix.

CHICKEN SCHNITZEL, FRIED EGG AND PARSLEY SALAD

There's a reason so many countries have their own version of schnitzel or escalope – it's such a homely treat and great fun to make.

SERVES 2

FOR THE CHICKEN
SCHNITZEL
2 chicken breasts, skinless
   and boneless
4 tbsp plain flour
salt and pepper
4 free-range eggs, beaten
60g fresh breadcrumbs
80g Parmesan, freshly grated
100g clarified butter or ghee
2 garlic cloves, peeled and
   left whole
a few fresh thyme sprigs

FOR THE PARSLEY SALAD
2 tbsp olive oil
2 tbsp red wine vinegar
1 tbsp caster sugar
1 large bunch flat-leaf parsley,
   leaves picked
1 tbsp chopped fresh dill
½ cucumber, thinly sliced
1 banana shallot, peeled and
   thinly sliced
1 large dill pickle, thinly sliced

TO SERVE
2 free-range eggs
2 tbsp vegetable oil
10g salted butter
1 lemon, cut into wedges

Lay the chicken between two sheets of greaseproof paper and use a rolling pin to flatten them to around 5mm thickness.

Put the flour in a wide, shallow bowl and season with salt and pepper. Put the beaten egg into a second bowl. Combine the breadcrumbs and grated Parmesan in a third bowl. Dip the chicken breasts in the flour, then the egg and then the breadcrumbs.

Heat the clarified butter in a frying pan over a fairly high heat and fry the chicken breasts for 3 minutes on each side until golden. Add the garlic and thyme once the chicken breasts are turned over in the pan, and baste. Remove the breasts from the pan, set aside to drain on kitchen paper and keep warm.

To make the parsley salad, mix together all the ingredients in a bowl and set aside.

Fry the eggs to your liking in a combination of vegetable oil and butter.

Put the schnitzel on plates, top with the fried eggs and serve with the parsley salad and lemon wedges.

ROAST CHICKEN WITH BAY LEAVES AND PRESERVED LEMONS

This is a great one-pot dish, which should take little over an hour to cook, and elevates the humble chicken to new heights! The preserved lemon can be picked up at most good supermarkets now — don't substitute it with a regular lemon. The saltiness the preserved ones bring is integral to this dish.

SERVES 4-6

4–5 whole preserved lemons
   (small, shop-bought ones)
1 large free-range chicken
salt and pepper
1 bunch fresh basil
1 twig bay leaves
extra virgin olive oil
2 garlic bulbs, cut in half
   horizontally
a few slices of grilled ciabatta
   or baguette

Preheat the oven to 200°C/400°F/Gas 6.

To start, halve the preserved lemons, scoop out the insides and keep the skins.

Season the chicken inside and out and stuff with the lemon skins, the basil and bay leaves. Rub with olive oil and put in a roasting tin.

Roast in the preheated oven with the garlic scattered around the bird for at least an hour, basting regularly. Check after an hour and allow longer depending on the size of the bird, but generally no more than another 20 minutes. To check if the chicken is cooked, insert a skewer into the flesh — if the juices that run out are transparent it is done, and if the juices are pink it needs longer.

When the chicken is cooked, allow to rest somewhere warm, and catch any resting juices. Leave for at least 15 minutes.

When ready to serve, remove the lemons from the cavity and smear the roasted garlic onto the grilled toasts (it should be rather molten). Chop up some of the preserved lemon and scatter over the garlic toast. Flash through the oven to warm while you are slicing the chicken. Serve the chicken over the garlic toast with the juices from the roasting tin.

PORK CHOP NORMANDE

I like to use veal chops for this classic Normandy-style dish, but they are
hard to find, and good-quality pork is a great alternative. All the cream,
apples and bacon make this a real hearty feast.

SERVES 2

FOR THE PORK CHOPS
2 tbsp olive oil
2 free-range pork chops
salt and pepper
1 tsp chopped fresh thyme leaves
1 garlic clove, peeled
15g unsalted butter
25ml Madeira

FOR THE GARNISH
25g unsalted butter
1 onion, peeled and thinly sliced
1 bay leaf
2 Braeburn apples, peeled
   and sliced
200g streaky bacon, diced
1 tbsp plain flour
300ml cider
50ml double cream
1 heaped tbsp crème fraîche
25ml Calvados
a handful of fresh parsley, chopped

Preheat the oven to 220°C/425°F/Gas 7.

To cook the pork, heat the oil in an ovenproof frying pan. Season the
chops well on both sides and fry them along the fat side to crisp up the
skin. Then fry the chops for 3–4 minutes on each side until browned.
Add the thyme and garlic and place in the oven for 6–8 minutes, or
until cooked to your liking.

Remove the pork from the oven and add the butter and Madeira to the
pan, stirring and scraping the pan with a wooden spoon. Baste the pork
chops with this mixture while they rest for 5–10 minutes.

To make the garnish, melt the butter in a saucepan over a medium heat
and fry the onions, bay, apples and bacon until lightly browned and
soft. Stir in the flour and mix well. Add the cider and cook to reduce
by about half, then add the cream and crème fraîche. Bring to the boil,
then add a splash of Calvados to taste, and then the parsley.

To serve, slice the chops and serve with the garnish on the side.

TARTIFLETTE

This always takes me back to skiing holidays with the kids, a naughty
dish of potato and Alpine cheese to help you warm up and dry off when
you come in off the slopes. The perfect winter treat in any cold climate.

SERVES 4

500g Maris Piper potatoes, peeled
1 bay leaf
salt
300g diced pancetta
3 tbsp olive oil or goose or duck fat
1 onion, peeled and sliced
3 garlic cloves, peeled and sliced
150ml white wine
250ml double cream
450g reblochon cheese

TO SERVE
cornichons
green salad
charcuterie

Put the potatoes into a pan with the bay leaf and some salt and bring to
a boil. Turn the heat off and leave for 5 minutes.

Remove and drain. When cool enough to handle, slice the potatoes
into thickish slices. If they break up a bit it doesn't matter too much.
Set aside.

Sweat the pancetta in a large pan with the olive oil before adding the
onions and garlic. Continue to sweat for another 15 minutes until
soft before pouring in the wine. Allow to evaporate before adding the
cream. Bring to a simmer and take off the heat.

Add the thinly sliced potatoes to the pan and carefully coat them in the
mix. Tip half the mix into a baking dish and add half the sliced cheese.
Tip over the rest of the potatoes and cover with the remainder of the
cheese. Bake at 180°C/350°F/Gas 4 for around 20–30 minutes until
golden and bubbling.

Allow to cool a little before serving with cornichons, a simple green
salad and perhaps some charcuterie on the side.

Photographed overleaf

PORK LOIN COOKED IN MILK, BAY AND LEMON

This is a beautifully gentle way of cooking a loin of pork. It's a traditional Italian method – the milk will curdle during the cooking process but the resulting juices are simply delicious. Serve with mashed potato or soft polenta.

SERVES 4-6

1 whole loin best-quality Old
   Spot pork, 1.5–2kg in weight,
   boneless and skinless
salt and pepper
olive oil
2 white onions, peeled and cut
   into quarters
100g unsalted butter
2 garlic bulbs, cut in half
1 bunch sage
approx. 2 litres milk (enough to
   cover the pork)
3 bay leaves
pared zest and juice of
   2 unwaxed lemons

Preheat the oven to 150°C/300°F/Gas 2.

Season the pork all over and seal in a little olive oil in a deep casserole or roasting tray big enough to hold the pork as a whole. Add the onions, butter, garlic and sage and let the pork sizzle to extract the flavour. Add the milk almost to cover, along with the bay leaves, lemon zest and half of the juice. Put into the low preheated oven and cook uncovered for $1^{1}/_{2}$–2 hours until the bones pull away easily.

Remove the pork and keep warm. Skim any excess fat from the sauce, taste and pour in the remaining lemon juice. On the hob, reduce to a sauce consistency. The sauce should now be nicely curdled.

Cut the meat into slices and spoon over the sauce and soft onions.

HAM HOCK, MUSTARD FRUITS AND FRESH HERB SAUCE

Ham hock is relatively inexpensive and, like other similar cuts, should be slow-cooked. The time invested is well worth the trouble. This is incredibly simple, but delivers the most delicious results and utilises the cooking liquor that is so often discarded.

You could make the mustard fruits (mostarda di cremona) yourself but it is time-consuming and there are some exceptionally good bottled varieties around. If you really want to push the boat out, I love to serve this dish with a few pan-fried scallops thrown in just before serving.

SERVES 4-6

2 salted ham hocks
4 celery sticks, cut in half
3 carrots, cut down the middle
 lengthways
2 large white onions, peeled
 and halved
1 twig bay leaves
3-4 cloves
1 tsp black peppercorns
1 garlic bulb, cut in half
a handful of parsley stalks
3-4 sprigs fresh thyme
400g jar mustard fruits (bottled
 is fine), to serve

FOR THE FRESH HERB SAUCE
1 tbsp red wine vinegar
1 tbsp Dijon mustard
6 tbsp extra virgin olive oil,
 plus extra to bind
½ bunch each fresh tarragon,
 mint, basil and flat-leaf
 parsley, chopped
1 tbsp capers
1 red onion, peeled and diced
salt and pepper

Put the ham hocks in cold water in a saucepan and bring to the boil. Boil for 1 minute, remove and change the water. Cover again in cold water and repeat the process twice more. This will rid the ham of any excess salt.

Throw the veg in the pan along with all the aromatics and bring to the boil. Simmer for 1½–2 hours or more or until the small bone at the top of the hock can be pulled free. Remove from the heat and allow the ham to cool in the stock.

When cool enough to handle, pick over the meat and remove any excess fat and sinew. Keep the meat in nice big chunks, do not shred. Set aside.

Take about 2–3 ladles of the cooking liquor, about 500ml, and pour through a fine-meshed sieve. Reduce in a pan by half to concentrate the flavours. Cool this stock in the fridge until required.

To make the herb sauce, mix the red wine vinegar, Dijon mustard and about 6 tablespoons extra virgin olive oil in a bowl. Stir in the herbs, capers and the onion. Season and add more olive oil to bind. Allow to mingle at room temperature for a while to improve the flavours.

When ready to serve, simply heat the reduced stock, and put the ham in it. Simmer for a few minutes and serve with some mustard fruits and a spoon of the herb sauce.

BRAISED LAMB BELLY

Lamb belly is a part of the animal that is often overlooked. It gives a delicious flavour and melting texture, with the added bonus of being one of the cheapest cuts available. Serve with caper mustard vinaigrette, tartare sauce or something with a tartness that will cut through the richness of the lamb.

SERVES 4

50g unsalted butter
25ml olive oil
2 lamb bellies. 900g–1kg each
salt and pepper
2 white onions, peeled and diced
2 carrots, diced
½ head of celery, diced
1 garlic bulb, cut in half
1 tbsp tomato purée
2–3 bay leaves
2–3 rosemary sprigs
200ml red wine
1 tbsp red wine vinegar
500ml lamb stock (see page 224)
    or water
caper mustard vinaigrette or
    tartare sauce, to serve

In a large casserole or saucepan, melt the butter and olive oil together. Season the lamb generously, add it to the pan and seal on all sides until golden. Remove from the pan.

Add the vegetables to the pan, including the garlic bulb, and sauté until golden, about 20–25 minutes. Stir in the tomato purée, bay leaves, rosemary, red wine and red wine vinegar. Put the lamb back into the pan and cover with the stock or water.

Bring to the boil, cover and simmer for 1½–2½ hours until tender. Remove the lamb carefully from the pan and place between two heavy baking trays to keep it flat. Refrigerate overnight.

The next day, gently remove the bones from the meat and cut the flesh into fingers. These can either be reheated in the stock and eaten as is, or they can be dipped in flour, egg and breadcrumbs and deep-fried or oven-baked until golden.

Serve with a caper mustard vinaigrette or tartare sauce and a bowl of seasonal leaves.

ROASTED LAMB CUTLETS WITH COCKLE VINAIGRETTE

I love the combination of textures and flavours here. It's a seriously delicious dish inspired by the best ingredients that Wales has to offer.

SERVES 2

6 lamb cutlets
salt and pepper
dash olive oil
30g salted butter
2 small sprigs rosemary
6 wild garlic leaves, if in season

FOR THE BLACKENED LEEKS
AND COCKLE VINAIGRETTE
1 leek, white part only, trimmed
olive oil
1 banana shallot, peeled
    and chopped
few sprigs fresh thyme
1 bay leaf
100ml Amontillado sherry
    or dry Madeira
250g cockles in shell
splash sherry vinegar

Preheat the oven to 220°C/425°F/Gas 7.

For the roasted lamb cutlets, season the lamb well with salt and freshly ground black pepper. Heat a dash of olive oil in a frying pan on high heat, add the lamb and cook until coloured on both sides, the skin is golden brown and the fat is crisp. Add the butter, rosemary and wild garlic and baste (spoon the butter back over the meat as it melts). Cover and leave to rest in a warm place.

To make the blackened leeks and cockle vinaigrette, rub the leek all over with 1 tablespoon of olive oil, season with salt and pepper and place in a roasting tin. Roast for about 20 minutes, until blackened all over and soft in the middle. Remove from the oven and set to one side as it continues to steam.

Heat a dash of olive oil in a frying pan with a lid, add the shallot, thyme and bay leaf and cook over a medium heat until the shallot has softened. Pour in the sherry and the cockles and immediately cover with a lid. Steam the cockles for a minute. Once cooked, strain and keep the cooking liquid. When cool enough to handle, pick the cockles from their shells. Discard any cockles that do not open.

Mix the strained liquid with 2 tablespoons of olive oil and a splash of sherry vinegar in a small bowl. Taste and season with salt and pepper.

To serve, arrange the cutlets on a plate and top with the wild garlic, then split open the blackened leek and spoon over some cockles and the vinaigrette.

RACK OF LAMB WITH BABY GEM LETTUCE, PEAS, MINT AND BACON

I don't really need to comment much on this one – it's heavenly, early summer on a plate!

SERVES 4

olive oil
2 x 8-bone racks of lamb
salt and pepper
4 sprigs fresh thyme, leaves picked
75g unsalted butter
4 medium baby gem lettuces, halved
200g pancetta or bacon, diced
4 garlic cloves, peeled and
  thinly sliced
100g fresh shelled peas, blanched
  and refreshed
800ml lamb stock (see page 224)
4 sprigs fresh mint, leaves picked
  and torn, plus extra to garnish

Preheat the oven to 200°C/400°F/Gas 6.

Heat 1 tablespoon of olive oil in a large frying pan. Season the lamb fat with salt and pepper, then fry fat side down for a few minutes over a high heat until browned.

Turn over, put into a roasting tin and sprinkle with some of the fresh thyme. Roast in the preheated oven for 15–20 minutes or to your liking. Leave to rest for 10 minutes before serving.

In another frying pan, add 15g of the butter and colour off the baby gem lettuces, cut side down, in the foaming butter. Throw in the diced pancetta, the garlic and remaining thyme, and sauté for a few minutes until coloured. Add the peas and pour in the lamb stock. Bring to the boil and simmer for 2–3 minutes to warm everything through.

Cut the lamb into chops and place on a large serving dish. Throw the mint into the simmering stock along with the remaining butter. Stir in to enrich the sauce and give it a good sheen. Season carefully, as the pancetta may already have seasoned the stock sufficiently. Spoon around the lamb racks and serve garnished with the extra mint.

RUMP OF WELSH LAMB, WITH SPICED AUBERGINE, MINT AND YOGHURT

This dish is based on the now classic vegetarian dish imam bayildi, which is delicious on its own, but works equally well with lamb. Serve with the flatbreads on page 228.

SERVES 4

4 lamb rumps or chumps
a few sprigs fresh rosemary
6 garlic cloves, peeled and
    left whole
knob of salted butter
3 aubergines
50ml olive oil, plus a little extra
salt and pepper
2 onions, peeled and diced
1 tsp ground allspice
½ tsp ground cumin
a pinch of cayenne pepper
100g currants
400g can chopped plum tomatoes
4–5 fresh plum tomatoes,
    roughly chopped
½ bunch each of fresh coriander
    and mint, chopped
flatbreads, to serve (see page 228)

FOR THE MINT YOGHURT
1 garlic clove, peeled
a few sprigs fresh mint,
    leaves picked
salt and white pepper
4 tbsp Greek yoghurt

Preheat the oven to 200°C/400°F/Gas 6.

Put the lamb in a roasting tin and roast in the preheated oven until pink, about 10–12 minutes. When out of the oven and resting, throw the rosemary sprigs, 2 of the garlic cloves and a knob of butter into the roasting tin, and baste from time to time.

Dice the aubergines into 1cm cubes. In a frying pan over a medium heat, fry the aubergine in the olive oil for 10–15 minutes until golden brown all over and soft. Season lightly with salt. Set aside.

In a saucepan, over a low heat, add some olive oil and sweat off the diced onion with the remaining whole garlic cloves. When translucent, after 10 minutes or so, add the spices and fry them off for 1 minute. Throw in the currants and canned tomatoes and cook for a further couple of minutes. Stir in the fresh tomatoes, followed by the aubergine chunks. Check the seasoning and add the freshly chopped herbs. Set aside.

Make the mint yoghurt by crushing the garlic clove and fresh mint along with a little salt and white pepper in a pestle and mortar. Stir this into the yoghurt and allow the flavours to mingle in the fridge.

Cut the lamb into thickish slices. Arrange next to a pile of aubergine, and spoon the yoghurt dressing over. Serve with warm flatbreads.

LAMB'S LIVER, BORLOTTI BEANS AND SHERRY VINAIGRETTE

It's important to always use the best-quality liver you can. The acidity of the sherry vinegar is an essential element here, as it acts as a balance against the richness of the liver. If you can't get fresh beans, there are plenty of great tinned and jarred ones available.

SERVES 2

25g salted butter
2 pieces lamb's liver, about 1cm
  thick and 200g each in weight
salt and pepper

FOR THE BEANS
about 200g podded fresh
  borlotti beans
1 onion, peeled and cut in half
1 carrot, whole
1 celery stick
1 garlic bulb, cut in half
3 bay leaves
10g fresh thyme leaves
smoked bacon scraps

FOR THE VINAIGRETTE
200ml mixed sunflower oil and
  peanut oil
50ml sherry vinegar
½ tsp Dijon mustard
½ garlic clove, peeled and crushed
3 fresh sage leaves, roughly chopped

First cook the borlotti beans. Put the beans, onion, carrot, celery, aromatics and bacon in a saucepan. Cover with cold water and simmer for 30–40 minutes until tender. Don't season until the end of cooking.

Make the vinaigrette by mixing the oil, vinegar, mustard and garlic together to emulsify before adding the fresh chopped sage.

To cook the liver, gently heat the butter in a frying pan until foaming. Season the liver and pan-fry over a medium heat for 2 minutes until the liver starts to colour. Turn over and cook for another minute. Remove and keep warm.

To finish the dish, drain the beans and dress with the vinaigrette. Place the liver on top and serve.

LAMB'S KIDNEYS IN BACON AND CABBAGE BROTH WITH THYME DUMPLINGS

Thoroughly tasty and warming – this is good, hearty comfort food.

SERVES 4

15g butter
8 lamb's kidneys, white fat and
    muscle tissue removed, sliced
    crossways 1cm thick
salt and pepper
fresh horseradish or mustard,
    to serve

FOR THE BROTH

2 white onions, peeled and diced
50g unsalted butter
150g good-quality farmhouse-style
    bacon, diced
1 garlic bulb, cut in half
a few sprigs fresh thyme
2–3 bay leaves
350g potatoes, peeled, diced and
    washed of starch
1.25 litres chicken or light lamb
    stock (see page 222 or 224)
1 Savoy cabbage, shredded

FOR THE THYME
DUMPLINGS

1 shallot, peeled and finely diced
30g butter
1 garlic clove, peeled and crushed
1 tbsp chopped fresh thyme leaves
100g shredded suet
100g self-raising flour
100g fresh breadcrumbs
2 medium free-range eggs, beaten

To make the broth, in a saucepan, sweat the onion gently in the butter until soft but not coloured. Add the diced bacon and continue to cook. Throw in the garlic, thyme and bay leaves, then stir in the diced potatoes. Cook for 5 minutes or so, then add 1 litre of the stock and bring to the boil. Simmer for 30 minutes. Season to taste.

Meanwhile, make the dumplings. In a frying pan, sweat the shallot in the butter until soft, then stir in the garlic and thyme and season. Mix this with the suet, flour and breadcrumbs. When cool enough, add the eggs. Mix together well. Roll into balls the size of pickled onions and poach very gently in the remaining hot chicken stock. The dumplings will take anywhere from 25 to 35 minutes, depending on the thickness. They should be slightly swollen and light to eat, not stodgy in any way.

Heat the butter in a frying pan on a medium–high heat until foaming. Season the kidneys and add to the foaming butter. Cook until lightly golden on both sides for no more than a minute each side. Remove from the heat and drain in a colander. Reserve somewhere warm until the bacon and cabbage broth is ready.

After the 30 minutes, stir the shredded cabbage into the broth and continue to simmer for a few minutes. Now drop in the kidneys and warm through gently for a minute or two. At this point it is very important not to boil the stock or the kidneys will toughen.

Serve the broth straight away with the thyme dumplings, and offer some fresh horseradish or mustard on the side.

BRAISED TOPSIDE WITH ANCHOVY AND ONION

I adapted this from Elizabeth David's classic cookbook *An Omelette and a Glass of Wine*. It is one of the easiest and tastiest recipes I know.

SERVES 4–6

300g unsalted butter, plus a
  little extra
6 white onions, peeled and cut
  thickly into half-moons
1–2kg beef topside, cut into
  portion-sized steaks
salt and pepper
2–3 bay leaves

FLAVOURINGS

2–3 garlic cloves, peeled
  and crushed
1–2 tbsp red wine vinegar
6 tbsp olive oil
5–6 anchovy fillets, chopped up
2 dried red chillies (bird's eye)
1 very large handful fresh
  flat-leaf parsley

Preheat the oven to 140°C/275°F/Gas 1.

Take a solid casserole with a lid, and rub all over the inside with the butter. Then scatter in some of the onions. Season the beef and add a layer over the onions. Continue to layer beef, onion and seasoning. Throw in the bay leaves. Smear a sheet of greaseproof paper with more butter, and place, butter-side down, on top of the meat and onions. Place the lid on the pot and heat over a medium heat until it starts to sizzle. Put into the preheated oven and leave for 2 hours, until the meat is very tender.

Place the rest of the ingredients – the flavourings – into a food processor, and blitz to make a paste. Stir the paste into the meat and juices. Replace the lid and leave to infuse for 30 minutes.

Gently reheat on the hob, and serve with mash and something green.

BRAISED BEEF RIB CURRY

A really satisfying, rich curry – perfect for a relaxed weekend treat.

SERVES 4

2kg beef short ribs, cut into
    2cm pieces

FOR THE MARINADE
½ tsp ground turmeric
½ tsp ground cinnamon
1 tsp ground cumin
1 tsp ground coriander
6 curry leaves, finely chopped
3 tbsp curry powder
3 garlic cloves, peeled and minced
2cm piece fresh ginger, peeled
    and finely grated

FOR THE CURRY
2 tbsp vegetable oil
1 onion, peeled and thinly sliced
4 garlic cloves, peeled and minced
2 lemongrass sticks, shredded
1 large aubergine, diced
2 green peppers, deseeded
    and diced
a handful of coriander, leaves and
    stalks separated, finely chopped
3 x 400g tins coconut milk
3 baby aubergines, halved
1 long violet aubergine, cut into
    strips (optional)
salt and pepper
1 lime, quartered

TO SERVE
cooked basmati rice
2 tbsp coconut flakes
sliced red chillies

Place the marinade ingredients in a bowl and mix well. Add the beef ribs and mix well to coat. Place in the fridge to marinate for 12 hours.

In a large frying pan, sear off the beef ribs, to colour all over.

Heat the vegetable oil in a large saucepan with a lid and cook the onions, garlic, lemongrass, aubergine, peppers and coriander stalks over a medium heat for 10 minutes. Add the ribs and marinade to the pan along with the coconut milk, cover with a lid and cook on a low heat for 3 hours, until the ribs are soft.

Add the rest of the aubergines and cook for another hour until soft, adding some water to the pot if necessary. Season the curry to taste with salt and pepper and stir in the coriander leaves.

Heat a griddle pan over a high heat and cook the lime quarters until charred. Serve the curry with cooked basmati rice, some coconut flakes and sliced red chillies, and the charred limes.

BRAISED OXTAIL WITH SEVILLE ORANGE

This oxtail is so tasty. It can be served with a very simple, traditional garnish like mash and greens, or you can layer the braised meat between sheets of lasagne for a slightly lighter dish.

SERVES 4

8 large oxtail chunks, bone in
1 bottle rich, deep red wine
a few black peppercorns
1 bay leaf
1 small bunch fresh thyme
1 garlic bulb, cut in half
2 star anise
olive oil
seasoned plain flour
2 large white onions, peeled
    and diced
4 celery sticks, diced
4 carrots, diced
pared zest and juice of 2
    Seville oranges
water, beef or chicken stock (see
    page 222), to cover

Put the oxtail pieces in a dish and add the red wine with the peppercorns, bay, thyme, garlic and star anise. Marinate overnight, covered, in the fridge The next day, drain the oxtail and reserve the red wine and aromatics.

Preheat the oven to 140°C/275°F/Gas 1.

Heat a film of oil in a large frying pan. Dust the oxtail in seasoned flour and fry off to seal the meat and colour on all sides. Remove from the pan. Throw in the diced veg, and colour these off too. This should take 10–20 minutes. Put the oxtail back in the pan with the reserved red wine and aromatics. Cook until reduced by half.

Add the Seville orange juice and zest and the stock or water to cover the oxtail and cook in the preheated oven until tender and the meat pulls away from the bone without much resistance. This will take anywhere from 2–4 hours, so be patient!

When cool enough to handle, pick the meat from the bones, discarding the fat if you prefer. Drain the stock, discarding the vegetables, but rescue the orange zest, which is now soft enough to eat. Bring the stock up to the boil and reduce by half. Reserve.

Serve the meat reheated in the sauce with the cooked orange zest.

GRILLED VENISON SKEWERS, WITH REDCURRANT DRESSING

With a rich meat like venison you need a zesty dressing, and this redcurrant and orange one is just the ticket.

SERVES 4

1 tsp black peppercorns, crushed
2 juniper berries, crushed
1 tsp chopped fresh thyme leaves
2 tbsp olive oil
500g venison haunch, cut
   into chunks

FOR THE SALAD
100g broad beans (podded weight)
2 baby gem lettuces, roughly
   chopped
3 spring onions, finely chopped
½ fennel bulb, thinly sliced
4 radishes, halved

FOR THE REDCURRANT
DRESSING
1 tbsp olive oil
1 shallot, peeled and finely chopped
1 small garlic clove, peeled and
   finely chopped
juice of 1 orange
1 tsp clear honey
1 tsp Dijon mustard
1 loose handful redcurrants
2 tbsp raspberry vinegar
salt and pepper

Combine the crushed peppercorns, juniper berries, thyme leaves and oil in a shallow dish. Add the venison chunks and stir to allow the marinade to cover the meat. Leave to marinate for at least an hour.

To make the salad, first pod the broad beans. Bring a saucepan of water to the boil. Add the beans, cook for about 2 minutes and then transfer the beans to a bowl of cold water. Pop the bright green beans out of their skins by squeezing gently – a small sharp knife will also help.

Combine the remaining salad ingredients with the beans in a bowl.

To make the redcurrant dressing, in a frying pan on a medium heat, add the olive oil and fry the shallot and garlic briefly, then stir in the orange juice, honey and mustard, followed by the redcurrants. Warm for a minute or two before adding the vinegar and then remove from the heat. Taste, season with salt and freshly ground black pepper and add more oil if necessary.

Thread the chunks of venison onto skewers and cook on a hot griddle pan for 2–4 minutes on each side, or until cooked to your liking. Rest for 5 minutes before serving.

To serve, dress the salad with the dressing and divide between plates. Top with the venison skewers.

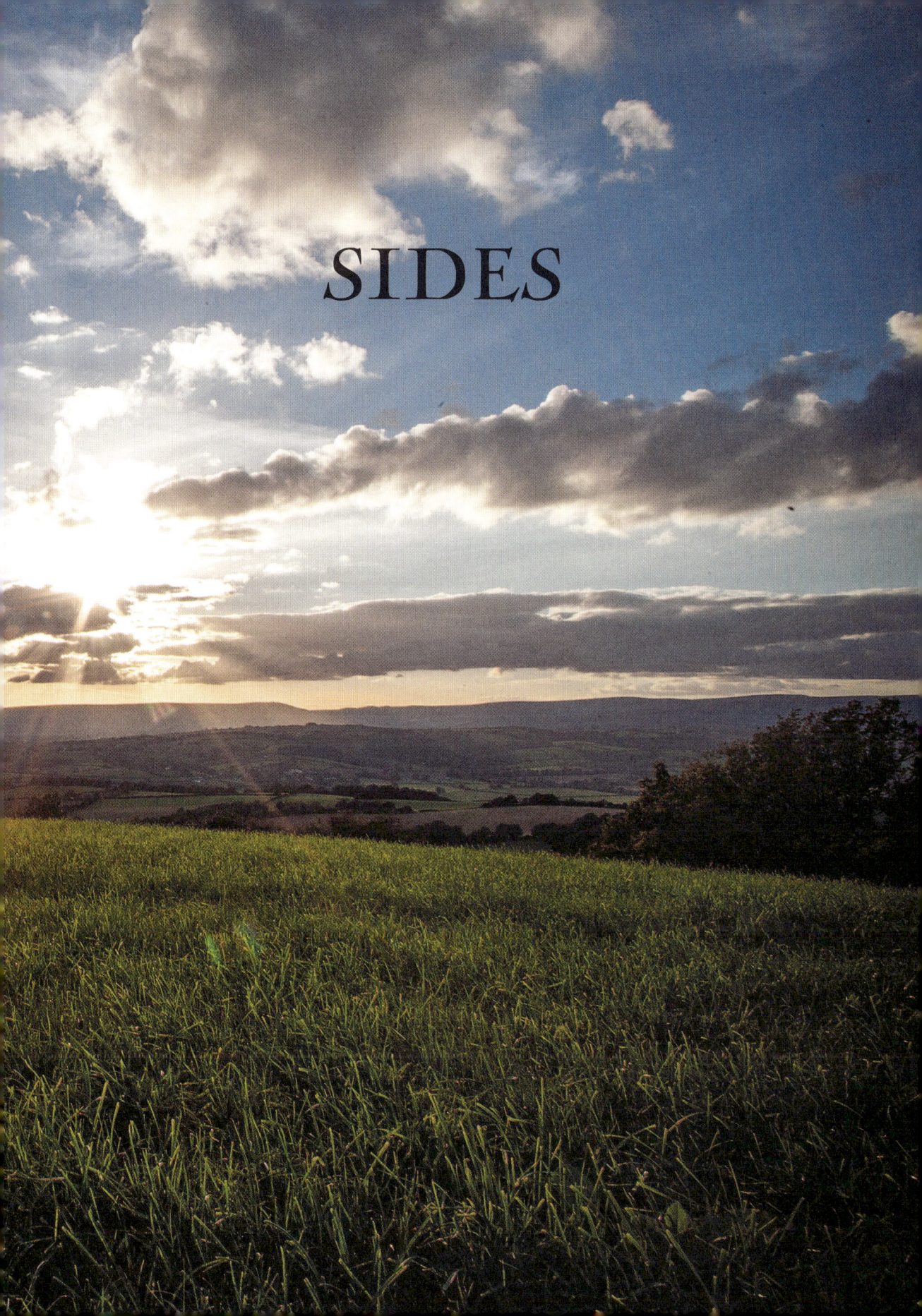

SIDES

DAUPHINOISE POTATOES

Either serve immediately or chill and use to make Savoyarde potatoes...
a delicious and quite naughty treat. Don't worry about all the cream and
butter, and don't try and reduce the quantities – that would spoil it. Just
don't eat it every day!

SERVES 4-6

100g salted butter, plus extra
    for greasing
250ml milk
250ml double cream
1 garlic bulb, cut in half
a few sprigs fresh thyme
3–4 bay leaves
salt and pepper
1kg floury potatoes (such as Maris
    Piper or Golden Wonder), peeled

Preheat the oven to 200°C/400°F/Gas 6, and butter a medium to large
ovenproof dish (the potatoes should be no more than 5cm high in
the dish).

Put the milk, cream, butter, garlic, thyme, bay leaves and some
seasoning into a saucepan and bring to the boil. Simmer for 10 minutes
to infuse the flavours.

Using a mandoline or very sharp knife, cut the potatoes into thin slices
(so they bend when stood up).

Strain the milk mixture. Put back into the pan and add the sliced
potatoes. Gently stir on the stove for 5–10 minutes to start cooking
and release the starch (this will help weld the Dauphinoise together
later). Tip into the buttered ovenproof dish with enough of the liquid
to just cover. Too much liquid would result in a delicious tasting but
sloppy dish.

Cook uncovered in the preheated oven for 20–30 minutes, until the
top starts to blister and colour. Turn the oven down to 150°C/300°F/
Gas 2, and continue to cook for another 40–50 minutes until a knife
will easily and without resistance go through the potatoes. Remove and
allow to rest a little before serving.

SAVOYARDE POTATOES

Potato in a wicked form. It's very difficult to limit yourself to one each,
so always make spares...

SERVES 4-6

1 recipe Dauphinoise potatoes
   (see opposite)
200g Fontina, Gruyère or
   Emmental cheese, grated
8 slices good-quality cured ham
700–800g puff pastry
1 medium free-range egg plus
   1 medium free-range egg yolk,
   beaten together, for glazing

Start with your Dauphinoise potatoes at room temperature. Using a small circular cutter, cut out 8 potato rounds from the dish. I usually use an upturned individual pudding mould or a coffee cup. Top each round with grated cheese and wrap around a piece of ham.

Roll out the pastry to the thickness of a pound coin and cut out 8 discs with a small side plate or saucer. Gently mould the pastry over the top of the potato and stretch to fit completely around each base. Pinch the pastry together and cut away any excess. Chill in the fridge for at least 30 minutes until ready to use.

Preheat the oven to 180°C/350°F/Gas 4. Line a baking sheet with baking paper.

Place the wrapped potatoes on the baking sheet, and glaze with the beaten egg. Cook for roughly 20 minutes until golden. Insert a skewer into the middle of the potato to check that it is hot.

With a sharp knife, cut each pastry casing down the middle to reveal the layers of potato, ham and cheese.

Photographed overleaf

ALIGOT WITH ROASTED ONIONS AND APPLES

You can experiment with different cheeses here, but you want something that melts easily and is a nutty, alpine style. This dish is a great accompaniment instead of your normal mash, but it can also stand alone as a warming meal.

SERVES 4

FOR THE ROASTED ONIONS
AND APPLES
6 round large shallots or small
    onions, peeled and slit ¾ of
    the way through
2 tbsp olive oil
50g unsalted butter
2 Cox's apples, quartered and cored
4 sage leaves, roughly chopped
1 bay leaf

FOR THE ALIGOT
1kg floury potatoes
6 garlic cloves, unpeeled and
    left whole
250ml whole milk
100ml double cream
150g salted butter
500g Cantal or Comté cheese, grated
white pepper, to taste

Preheat the oven to 200°C/400°F/Gas 6.

Bring a pan of salted water to the boil and boil the shallots or onions for 10 minutes to soften a little. Remove, drain and toss with the oil, butter, apples, sage and bay leaf in a roasting tin. Roast for 30 minutes until soft and caramelised.

To make the aligot, boil the potatoes and garlic in their skins until soft, then drain, peel the skins off and push both through a ricer.

Warm the milk, cream and butter in a pan and beat in the riced potato and garlic mixture and the grated cheese. Add some white pepper and continue to beat continuously, and for quite some time, until smooth.

Serve the cheesy mash alongside the roasted onions and apples.

POTATOES COOKED IN BAY AND MILK

A perfect summer Sunday lunch accompaniment. Use fewer bay leaves if you don't want too strong a flavour.

SERVES 6

100g salted butter
1kg small salad potatoes, scrubbed of their skins
salt and pepper
6–8 bay leaves, fresh or dried
about 850ml whole milk

Melt the butter in a large saucepan and throw in the potatoes and some seasoning. Colour gently all over for 10 minutes or so.

When the potatoes are nicely golden, add the bay leaves and milk, making sure the potatoes are covered. Gently simmer for 20 minutes until the potatoes are cooked through.

Turn off the heat and leave to infuse in the milk until ready to serve, then drain.

MASHED POTATO

This is special-occasion mash but definitely worth the extra effort.

SERVES 4 GENEROUSLY

8 large Maris Piper potatoes, peeled and quartered
salt, to taste
3 bay leaves
100g unsalted butter
200ml double cream

Rinse the potatoes of their starch under running water, or in several changes of water, for about 5 minutes.

Put into a large saucepan and cover with cold water. Add salt and the bay leaves, then bring to the boil and simmer until tender, which will take up to 30 minutes. Remove the potatoes from the water. Discard the bay leaves and steam-dry the potatoes for 5 minutes.

In a clean saucepan bring the butter and cream to the boil, then put to one side. Push the potatoes through a sieve and stir in the hot cream. Serve immediately.

BRAISED RED CABBAGE

This is a great seasonal staple. I often serve it with venison or some
rare roast beef. I'd avoid anything involving fish, though.

SERVES LOTS

3 large white onions, peeled
    and thinly sliced
50g salted butter
50ml extra virgin olive oil
salt and pepper
3 large Bramley apples, cored
    and cut into chunks
2 sprigs fresh rosemary
1 large red cabbage, cored
    and sliced
90g light brown sugar
100ml balsamic vinegar

In a large saucepan with a lid, sweat the onions down in the butter and
olive oil. At this point season with salt and pepper but don't allow the
onions to colour. Throw in the sliced Bramley apples and the rosemary,
and stir around to break the apples down.

Now add the sliced red cabbage. This will almost certainly fill the
whole pan, but don't panic. After a few minutes of vigorously stirring,
the quantity will start to reduce. Cover the pan with a heavy lid to
stop the steam from escaping and turn the heat down low. The cabbage
will now take anywhere between 45 minutes to 1 hour. Check every now
and then and give it a stir. Don't let the cabbage stick and burn; if it
starts to stick, add a splash of water.

When the cabbage has broken down, stir in the sugar and caramelise
for a few minutes, then add the vinegar and reduce until it has all gone.
It won't take long. Taste and serve.

PICNIC MUSHROOMS

I can remember holidaying in France with my family and eating these
straight from the paper cups they sell in delicatessens. Every time
I make them, I'm transported back to cloudy Brittany skies.

MAKES 1KG

600ml red wine vinegar
300ml red wine
1 tbsp sea salt
2 sprigs fresh thyme
2 juniper berries, crushed
3 bay leaves
2–3 cloves
1kg small button mushrooms,
   cleaned
olive oil

Put the vinegar and wine in a non-reactive saucepan and add all the
aromatics. Heat to near boiling, then leave to infuse for 30 minutes.

Strain into a clean pan, add half the mushrooms and simmer for
10–15 minutes. Remove the mushrooms to a suitable container using
a slotted spoon. Put the remainder of the mushrooms in the spiced
liquid and simmer for the same length of time. Using a slotted spoon,
add to the container with the first batch.

Cover the mushrooms with olive oil until required. They will keep
for several months in the fridge quite happily. They are good at
room temperature with a juicy rare steak or eaten from a jar with a
cocktail stick.

PURPLE-SPROUTING BROCCOLI WITH AN ANCHOVY AND BASIL *SAUCE*

In my kitchen, anchovy has become a classic, and a necessary, salty accompaniment to one of the season's most notable vegetables. This anchovy sauce keeps well in the fridge and gets better with age. Serve with roast lamb or a suitably robust fish, like pollack or hake.

SERVES 4

360–400g purple-sprouting
    broccoli
salt

FOR THE SAUCE
3 garlic cloves, peeled
1 small red chilli
1 x 50g can anchovy fillets, drained
3 tsp red wine vinegar
½ bunch fresh basil, roughly
    chopped
6–8 tbsp extra virgin olive oil

Blanch the broccoli in a saucepan of boiling salted water for 2 minutes. Drain well.

Either blend all the sauce ingredients in a food processor, adding the olive oil slowly, or pound the ingredients in a pestle and mortar.

Spoon the sauce over the warm purple-sprouting broccoli, and serve.

ST GEORGE'S MUSHROOMS, WILD GARLIC AND BACON

Just great country ingredients together on a plate. This dish would go well with a plate of freshly fried eggs.

SERVES 4

8 thick rashers of bacon, either streaky or back
50g unsalted butter
1 garlic clove, peeled and finely sliced
400g fresh St George's mushrooms
1 large handful of fresh, clean wild garlic leaves

In a frying pan, fry the bacon in the butter until crisp and coloured. Remove and keep warm. Throw the garlic slivers into the pan, sizzle for 1 minute until golden, then add the mushrooms and sauté for 2–3 minutes until cooked.

Cut the bacon into edible slices (this dish is a fork job only), put into the pan and add the wild garlic leaves. Stir to wilt the leaves and serve.

DESSERTS

SEVILLE ORANGE MARMALADE TART

The bitter Seville oranges marry perfectly with the sweet almondy flavours. This is essentially a jumped-up Bakewell tart!

SERVES 4-6

20cm pastry tart shell, uncooked
2–3 tbsp good-quality Seville
  orange marmalade
30g flaked almonds
clotted cream, to serve

FOR THE FRANGIPANE
250g unsalted butter
250g caster sugar
250g ground almonds
4 medium free-range eggs

To make the frangipane, beat or cream the butter and sugar in a food processor until the sugar has dissolved and the butter is pale. Turn the food processor speed down and add the ground almonds. Beat until just incorporated, then add the eggs one at a time so the mix doesn't split. Chill the frangipane until ready to use.

Preheat the oven to 150°C/300°F/Gas 2.

To assemble the tart, spread the marmalade on the base of the tart shell. Cover with the frangipane, sprinkle over the almonds and bake in the preheated oven for 40 minutes or until the frangipane is set (an inserted knife should come out clean).

Serve warm with a dollop of clotted cream.

RICE PUDDING TARTLETS

I discovered these little Italian tartlets, for which you will need four
13 x 3cm tartlet tins, in Venice. They are simple to make and very
delicious. Perfect with a strong coffee or glass of dessert wine.

MAKES 4 TARTLETS

FOR THE PASTRY
125g salted butter
100g icing sugar, plus extra
    for dusting
2 free-range egg yolks
250g Italian 00 plain flour,
    plus extra for dusting

FOR THE FILLING
25g unsalted butter
1 vanilla pod, split lengthways
40ml vin santo dessert wine
100g Arborio rice
500ml whole milk
60g caster sugar
a few strips of unwaxed orange peel
2 free-range egg yolks

To make the pastry, blitz the butter, icing sugar and egg yolks together
in a food processor. Add the flour and bring together into a dough.
Wrap in clingfilm and refrigerate until cold.

Preheat the oven to 210°C/410°F/Gas 6½.

Roll out the pastry and cut into four circle shapes, slightly larger than
the 13 x 3cm tartlet tins. Place the pastry circles into the tins and prick
each with a fork. Line the pastry shells with a scrunched-up piece of
baking paper and baking beans or rice. Blind bake for 10–15 minutes
and set aside to cool slightly before removing the paper and the beans.
Leave the oven on.

To make the filling, melt the butter in a saucepan with the vanilla and
the vin santo. Stir in the rice, then add in the milk, sugar and orange
peel. Cook on a low–medium heat for 40–50 minutes, until the rice is
tender and almost all of the milk has been absorbed. Remove from the
heat and carefully take out the vanilla pod and pieces of orange peel.
Quickly beat in the egg yolks.

Spoon the mixture into the cooked tartlet shells. Bake for 10–15
minutes until the filling is set and coloured. Dust each tartlet with
icing sugar and serve with a double shot of espresso or a glass of
vin santo.

GOOSEBERRY CRUMBLE TART

It is a shame that gooseberries are not more popular because the British
climate is particularly suited to producing perfect berries – juicy,
very tart and full of flavour. At the start of the season, gooseberries
are at their best for cooking, and there's no need to try and use them
for anything more complicated than a good old-fashioned gooseberry
tart or crumble. Later into the summer, when the sweeter, dessert
gooseberries are available, a straightforward fruit salad is a real seasonal
treat. This is another one inspired by my old boss Alastair Little.

SERVES 12

600g fresh gooseberries
150ml sweet dessert wine
125g caster sugar, or more to taste
1 vanilla pod, split lengthways
pared zest of 1 unwaxed orange
a few fresh elderflower heads,
    if in season, or a good dose of
    elderflower cordial, say 200ml
fresh cream or ice cream, to serve

FOR THE CRUMBLE TOPPING

50g blanched almonds
60g Italian 00 plain flour
a pinch of salt
40g quick-cook polenta
50g caster sugar
2 drops vanilla extract
75g chilled unsalted butter, chopped

FOR THE PASTRY

280g plain flour, plus extra
    for dusting
a pinch of salt
230g unsalted butter, softened
2 medium free-range egg yolks
1 vanilla pod, split lengthways
    and seeds scraped
115g icing sugar
finely grated zest of 1 unwaxed
    lemon (optional)

Preheat the oven to 180°C/350°F/Gas 4.

Top and tail the gooseberries and rinse. In a large saucepan with a
lid, put the sweet wine, sugar, vanilla pod and scraped seeds, orange
zest and elderflower and bring to the boil. Leave to infuse for a few
minutes, then add the gooseberries. Cover with a lid, pull off the stove
and let the fruit sit in the hot liquid until soft. This method will ensure
the gooseberries do not explode when cooking.

To make the crumble, in a dry frying pan, toast the almonds, then
remove and chop finely. Mix with the flour, salt, polenta, sugar and
vanilla extract. Rub in the butter and spread out over a tray. Chill for
30 minutes to firm up. Bake in the preheated oven for 30–40 minutes.
Remove and allow to cool. Break up with your hands and set aside.

Meanwhile, to make the pastry, mix the flour and salt together. Make a
well in the centre and add the soft butter, egg yolks, vanilla seeds, icing
sugar and lemon zest, if using. Combine, then roll into a log shape and
wrap. Chill for at least an hour.

Remove the pastry from the fridge and dust a 30cm tart tin with extra
flour. Cut the log of pastry into 1cm circles and arrange in the tin –
butting the edges of the circles together and pressing the edges to seal.
(As the pastry is sugary, this keeps it short and prevents over-rolling.)
Chill for 10 minutes. Blind-bake the tart shell (with the tart tin lined
with greaseproof paper and baking beans) in the preheated oven for
20–25 minutes, at the same temperature as above, until golden brown.

Drain the gooseberries (take out the vanilla pod) and fill the pastry
case with them. Sprinkle over the crumble mix and reheat the whole
tart for 10–15 minutes at 150°C/300°F/Gas 2.

Serve with fresh cream or good-quality ice cream.

TOFFEE, HAZELNUT AND WHISKY TART

Three of my favourite things in one dish!

SERVES 8-10

100g hazelnuts
120g caster sugar
25–50ml whisky
500ml double cream
7 free-range egg yolks
40g light brown sugar
18cm ready-made sweet pastry case

TO SERVE
400g fresh raspberries
2 tbsp whisky
400g crème fraîche

Preheat the oven to 180°C/350°F/Gas 4.

Spread the hazelnuts over a baking tray and roast for about 15 minutes, or until nicely browned. Remove from the oven, cool slightly and roughly chop. Set aside.

Reduce the oven temperature to 140°C/275°F/Gas 1.

In a deep frying pan or saucepan, add the caster sugar and 3 tablespoons of water. Melt the sugar over a medium heat, watching it all the time. Don't stir it, but you can move the pan around in a swirling motion. The sugar syrup will boil and turn a dark caramel colour after about 5 minutes. Quickly pour in the whisky and double cream and set aside to cool.

Whisk the yolks and the brown sugar in a bowl until the sugar is dissolved and the mixture is fluffy. Pour the cooled whisky caramel over the yolks, stir to mix together and then strain through a sieve. Pour into the sweet pastry case. Bake the tart for 30–45 minutes, or until almost set. It should have a slight wobble in the middle.

Remove the tart from the oven and immediately scatter over the chopped hazelnuts so they stick to the top of the tart. Leave to cool to room temperature.

To serve, top the tart with fresh raspberries and sprinkle more whisky over the whole tart. Serve in slices with the crème fraîche on the side.

CUSTARD AND NUTMEG TART

Another British classic, and one I'm quite partial to...

SERVES 10

2 vanilla pods, split lengthways
1 litre double cream
10 medium free-range eggs, beaten
250g caster sugar
1 blind-baked 30cm pastry tart
    shell (see page 165)
nutmeg, to grate

Preheat the oven to 110°C/225°F/Gas ¼.

For the custard tart filling, scrape the vanilla seeds from the pods and add both the pods and seeds to the cream. In a saucepan, bring the cream and vanilla to the boil to infuse. Put the beaten eggs and sugar in a bowl, and pour over the warm cream, stirring well. Push through a sieve into a bowl.

Pour the mixture into the blind-baked pastry case and cook in the preheated low oven for about 1 hour or until it's just about to set. Now grate some fresh nutmeg over the top while it's still sticky. Return to the oven, with the door left open and the oven turned off. Allow the tart to set and cool before serving.

BREAD AND BUTTER PUDDING

Serve simply, good and warm, with clotted cream or, if possible, homemade custard (see page 207). You can of course make this with a panettone or leftover bread instead of croissants.

SERVES 6-8

5 medium free-range eggs
45g caster sugar
a pinch of salt
2 vanilla pods, split lengthways
300ml milk
300ml double cream
a handful each of mixed dried fruit
    and candied peel
4–6 croissants
250g unsalted butter

Put the eggs and sugar together in a bowl, add a pinch of salt and the scraped vanilla pods and seeds and whisk together, then pour in the milk and cream. Set to one side.

Generously scatter the dried fruit and candied peel into a deep 25 x 35cm ovenproof dish. Cut the croissants in half horizontally. Melt the butter and generously butter the croissants, then lay them in the dish, gently overlapping.

Now pour the custard mix over the top and fill to the top of the dish. There should be almost three times as much custard as bread when finished. You might not get all the custard in. Leave the pudding to stand for 30 minutes to absorb the liquid.

Preheat the oven to 150°C/300°F/Gas 2.

Pour any remaining custard into the pudding and press the croissants down with your hands to help cover them completely. They will bob around on top – this is fine. Cook in the preheated oven for 30 minutes or so until the pudding is firm with still a little give in the middle.

Turn the oven off and allow to rest with the door ajar. Serve warm.

FAR BRETON

You use a clafoutis-style base here for this northern French favourite.
I like to use cider brandy to soak the prunes, as this gives you a great
sauce to pour over when serving. Don't worry if it gets quite dark on top
during cooking.

SERVES 4-6

80ml cider brandy
200g prunes, stones removed
480ml whole milk
1 vanilla pod, split lengthways,
  seeds scraped
60g unsalted butter
3 free-range eggs
90g plain flour
100g caster sugar
400g crème fraîche, to serve

Place the brandy and prunes in a saucepan and bring to a simmer. Turn
off the heat and leave the prunes to cool in the liquid. Once cool, drain
the prunes and reserve the liquid.

Preheat the oven to 220°C/425°F/Gas 7.

Place the milk with the vanilla pod and seeds in a small saucepan over a
low heat and cook to infuse the milk for 5 minutes, then strain.

In a separate small saucepan or frying pan, heat the butter until it
turns a nut brown colour. Tip into a bowl and leave to cool.

Whisk the eggs, flour and sugar together in a bowl, then slowly add the
infused milk. Whisk in the cooled butter. Sieve the mixture to remove
any lumps.

Scatter the drained prunes into a 23cm baking dish and pour over the
batter mixture. Bake for 30–40 minutes until almost set, but still with
a wobble in the middle. Leave to cool to room temperature.

Serve with crème fraîche and spoonfuls of the prune soaking liquid.

BUTTERSCOTCH PUDDING WITH WHISKY SAUCE

I've used walnuts and prunes in this one. If this is not your thing, just leave them out. The whisky sauce, however, is essential to the decadence of the dish. Serve with lots of thick double cream.

SERVES 6-8

50g unsalted butter, plus extra
    for greasing
60g light brown sugar
1 vanilla pod, split lengthways,
    seeds scraped
2 tsp baking powder
225g self-raising flour
a pinch of bicarbonate of soda
2 medium free-range eggs
300ml milk, warmed
50g stoned prunes, chopped
50g shelled walnuts, chopped

FOR THE WHISKY SAUCE
85g salted butter
85g muscovado sugar
200ml double cream
whisky

Preheat the oven to 180°C/350°F/Gas 4. Grease a 20cm square baking tin.

In a bowl, beat the butter, sugar and vanilla seeds together. In another bowl, mix the baking powder with the self-raising flour and bicarbonate. Beat the eggs in a third bowl. Slowly and alternately add small amounts of flour and egg to the butter mixture until all is incorporated. Do not over-beat the flour as this will toughen the gluten and produce a dense cake. Add the milk to form a sloppy batter. Stir in the fruit and nuts. Pour the mix into the baking tin and cook in the preheated oven for 30–40 minutes until firm.

To make the sauce, boil the butter and sugar together for 5 minutes. Pour in the cream, bring back to the boil, then add a capful of whisky or two to taste.

To serve, cut out a wedge of the sponge pud and coat liberally with the whisky sauce.

CHOCOLATE AND PEAR TART

Don't be tempted to cut into the tart for a few hours, as the filling will
still be very molten. This is a very gooey chocolate tart even when set for
a few hours. If the pears don't appeal, it's delicious without them as a
straightforward chocolate tart.

SERVES 8-10

4 medium free-range eggs
180g caster sugar
250g unsalted butter
380g good dark chocolate,
  broken into pieces
4 poached pears, cut in
  half lengthways
4 tbsp Poire William (eau de vie)
1 blind-baked 30cm pastry tart
  shell (see page 165)
double cream mixed with a little
  icing sugar and Poire William,
  to serve

Preheat the oven to 140°C/275°F/Gas 1.

Whisk the eggs and sugar together until they have tripled in volume.

Meanwhile, melt the butter and chocolate together in a bowl over a pan
of hot water.

Toss the poached pears in the Poire William and leave them to steep for
a few minutes. Lay the poached pears cut side down around the base of
the tart shell, fat ends towards the edge.

Now carefully pour the chocolate and butter mix into the eggs and
sugar. Stop whisking and gently pour the chocolate mix over the pears.
Immediately put into the oven and bake for 10–15 minutes until small
cracks start to appear around the outside of the chocolate. Remove
from the oven and cool.

Serve with a big dollop of cream flavoured with a little icing sugar and
Poire William.

SPICED APPLE TARTE TATIN WITH CLOTTED CREAM

This is my daughter's favourite pudding, a spiced-up version of the classic French dessert, and one of the first things I learned to cook. It takes a while to master and requires investment in a really good pan, but it's well worth the effort. You'll never have any leftovers serving this dish!

SERVES 2-4

3 Cox's apples, peeled and halved
100g unsalted butter, softened
100g caster sugar
1 cinnamon stick
1 star anise
1 vanilla pod, split lengthways
a twist of black pepper
a pinch of freshly grated nutmeg
flour, for dusting
200g puff pastry
clotted cream, to serve

Peel and core the apples, then cut in half from top to bottom. Set aside.

Press the butter into the base of a 20cm-diameter ovenproof copper or heavy-based pan with the back of a wooden spoon until it melts to completely cover the base. Sprinkle over the caster sugar in an even layer. Place the cinnamon stick, star anise, vanilla pod, black pepper and nutmeg in the pan, then lay the halved apples on top, cut sides facing up.

On a floured surface, roll out the puff pastry to 3mm thick, then cut around a plate about 3cm larger than the cooking pan. Place the pastry in the pan, pushing it down between the side of the pan and the apples to create the sides of the tart. Make sure the whole pan is tightly packed. Prick the top all over to allow the steam to escape when cooking, then chill for 30 minutes or so.

Preheat the oven to 220°C/425°F/Gas 7.

To cook, put the pan over a moderate heat and every few minutes shake the pan to prevent the apples from burning. Look for a golden caramel colour to appear around the side of the pan, after about 6–8 minutes. (At this point, if the pastry starts to melt, you've rolled it too thin. Remove, cool and start again.) Bake in the oven for 20–25 minutes, until the pastry is firm and golden.

If you are not serving the tart immediately, you can leave it in the pan and reheat it later, or turn it out warm and serve with clotted cream.

MONMOUTH PUDDING

This is a traditional Welsh recipe from the part of Wales I live in. It's very similar to one of my all-time favourites, the nostalgic queen of puddings. A real treat for those with a sweet tooth.

SERVES 4-6

450ml milk
finely grated zest of 1 unwaxed
    lemon
2 tbsp caster sugar
25g salted butter
90g fresh breadcrumbs, toasted
    with a sprinkle of brown sugar
3 large free-range egg yolks

FOR THE TOPPING
150g frozen raspberries
about 200g raspberry jam,
    preferably homemade

FOR THE MERINGUE
3 large free-range egg whites
75g caster sugar

Preheat the oven to 150°C/300°F/Gas 2.

In a saucepan, simmer the milk, lemon zest, sugar and butter together. Stir in the toasted breadcrumbs and leave to stand for 30 minutes.

Stir the egg yolks into the breadcrumb mixture, then pour into a suitable ovenproof serving dish. Bake for 25–30 minutes until just set. Remove from the oven.

Put the oven temperature up to 180°C/350°F/Gas 4.

Scatter the raspberries over the pudding base, and spoon the jam over the raspberries.

In a clean bowl, whisk the egg whites until they form firm peaks. Fold in the sugar and whisk again until stiff. Spoon the meringue over the dish and return to the oven for 8–10 minutes until golden. Serve warm.

RHUBARB COMPOTE, BLOOD ORANGE CREAM AND GINGER ICE CREAM

If you dislike the colour of cooked rhubarb, you can retain the pinkness by adding a drop or two of Grenadine, but this is not necessary and won't give you the real feeling of homemade comfort food.

SERVES 4

FOR THE GINGER
ICE CREAM
250ml whole milk
300ml double cream
1 vanilla pod, split lengthways
    and seeds scraped
200g stem ginger, grated,
    with about 2 tsp of its syrup
    (or more, to taste)
3 medium free-range egg yolks
85g caster sugar

FOR THE RHUBARB
COMPOTE
200ml ginger wine
a few strips of unwaxed orange zest
75g soft light brown sugar
250g young pink rhubarb,
    cut into 3cm batons

FOR THE BLOOD
ORANGE CREAM
150ml double cream
1 recipe blood orange curd
    (see opposite)

For the ice cream, heat the milk, cream, vanilla seeds, ginger and syrup together in a saucepan. Whisk the egg yolks and sugar together in a bowl. Pour the milk mix over the eggs and sugar and return to the pan to thicken over a gentle heat.

Remove from the stove, cool, then churn in the usual way in an ice-cream maker. When almost done, remove and decant to the freezer.

For the compote, bring the ginger wine, zest and sugar to the boil in a saucepan. Turn the heat down, throw in the rhubarb, and cook gently until tender, no longer than 3–5 minutes. This is compote, so don't worry when the rhubarb starts to break down. Reserve the stewed fruit until later.

For the blood orange cream, whip the double cream to soft peaks and fold in enough of the curd to taste.

To assemble, sit a ball or dollop of ice cream in a bowl, spoon round the rhubarb and carefully spoon over some of the blood orange cream.

You could also serve this with homemade biscuits (see the recipes for amaretti or hazelnut shortbreads on pages 216 and 217).

BLOOD ORANGE CURD

You can use blood orange curd as you would lemon curd... so on toast or
to make a tart. I like to serve it, mixed with some double cream, with the
rhubarb compote and ginger ice cream opposite.

MAKES 350-400ML

about 4 blood oranges to give 150ml
    juice, and grated zest of 2
4 medium free-range egg yolks
100g caster sugar
75g unsalted butter, softened

Put the orange juice, grated zest, egg yolks and sugar in a large bowl
over a pan of boiling water, and whisk until thickened. Slowly add the
softened butter until fully whisked in. Chill until ready to use.

The curd will keep for a few weeks, covered, in the fridge.

VANILLA CREAM TART WITH BLUEBERRIES

I used to make this in the restaurant using local whimberries. They are quite time-consuming to pick in a sufficient quantity, but if you can find some, they really are the most delightful berry to use in cooking. Blueberries don't have quite the same delicate flavour, but they do work just as well in jazzing up an otherwise simple tart.

SERVES 6

400g puff pastry
flour, for dusting
2 vanilla pods, split lengthways,
 seeds scraped
1 litre UHT double cream
40–60g caster sugar

FOR THE BLUEBERRY
COMPOTE
300g fresh blueberries
caster sugar, to taste

To make the compote, warm the blueberries in a saucepan gently, with just enough sugar to sweeten slightly, probably about a teaspoon. The berries will release their juice and just about lose their shape. Pull off the heat and reserve.

Preheat the oven to 190°C/375°C/Gas 5.

To make the tart base, roll out the puff pastry ultra-thin on a floured surface, and use to line a 25cm tart tin. Chill for 15 minutes, then blind-bake (lined with greaseproof paper and baking beans) for 20 minutes.

Mix the vanilla pods and seeds into the UHT double cream and heat in a saucepan until reduced to a setting consistency, which will take about 8–10 minutes. It is important to keep stirring, otherwise the mix could catch on the bottom and turn bitter. Add the caster sugar to taste.

Pour this into the blind-baked tart shell, place in the fridge and allow to set overnight.

When ready to serve, glaze with a blowtorch (or under the grill). Serve at room temperature with the fruit compote.

TREACLE TART

This is one of my childhood favourites. I've incorporated a little grated apple into the filling, just to take the edge off the sweet syrup and lighten the texture.

SERVES 8

1 blind-baked 30cm pastry tart
    shell (see page 165)
a pinch of freshly grated nutmeg
clotted cream or custard, to serve

FOR THE FILLING
500ml golden syrup
finely grated zest and juice
    of 1 unwaxed lemon
150g brioche or croissant crumbs
250ml double cream
5 medium free-range eggs, beaten
1 Bramley apple, peeled and
    finely grated

Preheat the oven to 160°C/325°F/Gas 3.

Heat the golden syrup, lemon zest and juice together in a medium saucepan. Stir in the crumbs and the cream. Take off the heat and, when cool, add the eggs and the grated apple.

Pour into the pastry tart shell and bake in the preheated oven for 30–40 minutes or until the tart is fully set and shows no sign of wobble. As soon as it comes out of the oven, sprinkle the nutmeg over. Allow to cool.

Serve warm or cold with clotted cream or custard.

BLACKBERRY AND APPLE SUET PUDDING

I like to use suet puddings as a change from steamed puddings.
You get that little bit of crispiness and they're not so stodgy. You
can experiment with different fruit, but blackberry and apple make
a perfect seasonal pairing.

SERVES 6-8

250g self-raising flour
a pinch of salt
120g shredded suet
100ml milk, plus extra for brushing
290g blackberry jam
2 Cox's or Bramley apples, grated
custard (see page 207) or clotted
    cream, to serve

FOR THE SAUCE
60g unsalted butter
60g light brown sugar
60ml glucose syrup
2 tbsp water
90g flaked almonds

Preheat the oven to 200°C/400°F/Gas 6.

Sift the flour and salt into a bowl. Throw in the suet and add enough of
the milk to allow the mix to come together to a sticky dough. You might
need a little more or less.

On a floured surface, roll the dough out to a large rectangle about 1cm
thick. Spread over the jam and grated apple. Roll up lengthways.

Put the roll onto a baking tray, brush with a little milk and bake in the
oven for 35–40 minutes until cooked.

In a pan, bring the sauce ingredients to the boil together. Spoon this
mixture over the top of the pudding and put in the preheated oven for
another 10 minutes until golden. Serve with custard or clotted cream.

POACHED PEAR WITH HONEYCOMB AND BLUE CHEESE

The key thing here is the quality of the honeycomb and the
blue cheese – get it right, and they make a sublime combination.
I like to use a good Roquefort here.

SERVES 4

4 Conference pears
pared zest and juice of 2 unwaxed
    lemons
150ml white wine
150ml water
85g caster sugar
2 cinnamon sticks
a generous pinch of saffron strands
1 tbsp runny honey

TO SERVE
about 120g honeycomb
about 400g creamy blue cheese
    such as Roquefort, at room
    temperature

Peel the pears and set aside. Mix the remaining ingredients together
in a suitably sized pan and bring to the boil. Add the pears and simmer
for 20–30 minutes, depending on the ripeness of the fruit. Chill the
pears in the cooking liquor.

Remove the pears, and serve them with a chunk of gooey honeycomb
and a thick slice of good-quality blue cheese.

CHOCOLATE PUDDING AND MASCARPONE ICE CREAM

This is quite a light, delicate chocolate cake, with a deliciously molten interior. The star anise is optional if you're not a fan.

MAKES 10-12 LITTLE
PUDDINGS

FOR THE MASCARPONE
ICE CREAM
350ml water
150g caster sugar
finely grated zest and
   juice (about 75ml) of
   2 unwaxed lemons
400g mascarpone cheese

FOR THE CHOCOLATE
PUDDINGS
250g dark chocolate, broken
   into pieces
250g unsalted butter
125g caster sugar
1 tsp freshly ground star anise,
   sieved (remove the seeds from
   the pod, and crush in a pestle
   and mortar); optional
5 medium free-range eggs
5 medium free-range egg yolks
50g plain flour
a pinch of salt
good-quality cocoa powder,
   to serve (optional)

Start both the ice cream and cake the day before. For the ice cream, simply boil the water, sugar and lemon zest in a saucepan. Once the sugar has dissolved, remove from the heat and stir in the mascarpone with the lemon juice. Cool and chill in an ice-cream maker (be careful not to over-churn). Freeze in a suitable container.

For the chocolate pudding, melt the chocolate and butter in a bowl over a saucepan of hot water. In a bowl, whisk the sugar, powdered anise, whole eggs and egg yolks until light and pale. Slowly add the melted chocolate to the egg and sugar mixture. Carefully fold in the flour and salt. Pour the mixture into little 200ml non-stick moulds, filling them halfway. Chill in the fridge overnight.

Next day, preheat the oven to 180°C/350°F/Gas 4.

Remove the pudding batter from the fridge, bring to room temperature and bake in the preheated oven for 10 minutes, no longer. The outside of the cake mix should be set firm yet the middle will remain molten.

Serve the cake hot with the mascarpone ice cream and a dusting of cocoa powder, if liked.

ORANGE AND VANILLA BABA

I have very fond memories of eating rum babas, or 'savarins', as chefs like to call them, in scary 1970s restaurants. This is my version of that boozy treat using orange-based Grand Marnier.

SERVES 6

500g self-raising flour
10g salt
40g caster sugar, plus a little extra
20g fresh yeast
150ml warm water
6 medium free-range eggs, beaten
2 tsp milk, warmed
150g unsalted butter, softened
caramelised or fresh orange
    segments and Jersey cream,
    to serve

FOR THE GRAND
MARNIER SAUCE
130g caster sugar
500ml water
1 vanilla pod, split lengthways
130–150ml Grand Marnier (or dark
    rum, if you prefer)
finely grated zest of 2 unwaxed
    oranges (Seville if available)

For the rum baba, sift the flour, salt and 40g caster sugar into a large bowl. In a separate bowl, crumble the yeast into the warm water with a little more sugar. Stir the warm water and yeast into the flour, and mix. Slowly stir in the eggs, warm milk and softened butter until you have a smooth batter. When all has been brought together, cover the bowl with clingfilm and allow to prove for at least an hour.

Knock back the soft dough and knead for 10 minutes until smooth and springy. The dough should lose all of its cellulite appearance. Butter a 20–25cm ring mould and spoon in the dough. Leave to rise for 15 minutes.

Preheat the oven to 180°C/350°F/Gas 4.

Bake the rum baba for 30 minutes or so until the surface is golden and well risen, or a knife inserted comes out cleanly. Allow to cool in the tin. (You can also bake this in individual moulds, and cook for about 15 minutes.)

Meanwhile, make the sauce. In a small saucepan, bring the caster sugar to the boil with the water and vanilla pod. Boil only until the sugar has dissolved. Add the Grand Marnier to taste, along with the orange zest. (During the winter months this is best with the bitter Seville oranges or blood oranges when in season.) Remove the vanilla pod.

Finally, prick the baba all over, to better absorb the liquid. Place in a serving dish and pour over the sauce. Serve with some caramelised or fresh orange segments and some very thick Jersey cream.

PEANUT BUTTER PARFAIT AND CARAMEL SAUCE

One of my chefs showed me this recipe, back in the day.
It is utterly delicious.

SERVES 6-8

165g caster sugar
12 medium free-range egg yolks
220g chunky peanut butter
200g double cream
50ml dark rum
50g toasted and chopped peanuts,
    to serve

FOR THE CARAMEL SAUCE
250g caster sugar
250ml pourable double cream
250ml semi-whipped double cream

In a heavy-based saucepan, boil the caster sugar with 6 tablespoons water to the soft ball stage – 116°C/240°F. You will need a sugar thermometer for this to be accurate.

Meanwhile, whisk the yolks in a food processor until light and pale. When ready, pour the sugar syrup down the side of the mixer onto the eggs. The bowl will heat up at this point, so keep whisking until it cools.

Stir in the peanut butter. Whip up the double cream to soft peaks and fold this and the alcohol into the peanut mix. Freeze in a terrine mould for at least 24 hours.

To make the caramel sauce, heat the sugar in a dry pan until it liquefies and goes golden brown. Stop the caramelisation by pouring in the double cream, taking care not to spill any of this molten goo, as it is incredibly hot. Pour this into the semi-whipped cream and pass through a sieve.

Serve the parfait in slices with the warm caramel sauce and the toasted chopped peanuts.

VIN SANTO, PINE NUT AND OLIVE OIL CAKE

There are many versions of this classic olive oil cake recipe, and this one is essentially borrowed from Alastair Little's *Keep It Simple*, with a few small changes of my own. The success of the dish lies very much in the quality of the olive oil used.

SERVES 8–10

4 medium free-range eggs
125g caster sugar
finely grated zest of 1 unwaxed
    lemon and 1 unwaxed orange
125g plain flour, plus extra
    for dusting
6 tbsp vin santo
3 tbsp best-quality extra virgin
    olive oil, plus extra for greasing
50g pine nuts
icing sugar, for dusting
crème fraîche or fruit compote,
    to serve

Preheat the oven to 150°C/300°F/Gas 2. Grease and flour a 28cm cake tin.

In a food processor, whisk the eggs and sugar for about 10 minutes until pale. Add both the zests.

Sift the flour onto a piece of baking paper. Turn the food processor down, quickly slide in the flour and pour in the vin santo and olive oil. Turn off the machine and continue to gently fold the mix together with a spoon. Pour the mix into the prepared tin. Bake in the preheated oven for 25–35 minutes or until a knife inserted comes out clean. Remove the cake from the tin and allow to cool.

Scatter over the pine nuts, dust with icing sugar and glaze briefly with a blowtorch. Serve with crème fraîche or a fruit compote.

STRAWBERRIES, ORANGES, CAVA AND MINT

This ever-so-easy recipe makes a refreshing end to a summer lunch.
Feel free to use prosecco or champagne if you want to be extravagant...

SERVES 4

2 punnets strawberries
1 tbsp caster sugar
½ vanilla pod, split lengthways
    and seeds scraped
2 punnets wild strawberries
    (if available)
2 oranges, peeled and segmented
1 cucumber, deseeded and diced
2 bunches blackcurrants
2 bunches redcurrants
1 bunch fresh mint, roughly torn
750ml bottle cava

Take one punnet of the large strawberries and purée with the caster sugar and vanilla seeds. Sieve the sauce. Taste and add more sugar if necessary.

Pour some of the strawberry sauce into the bottom of four serving dishes. Arrange the rest of the fruit on top of the purée and scatter over the mint.

Pour the cava over each bowl of fruit at the table and allow to fizz about. Serve immediately.

RED WINE POACHED STRAWBERRIES, WITH CINNAMON TOAST

Ideally use a light, summer-drinking red, like a Fleurie or Pinot Noir,
to make the most of this dish.

SERVES 4

900g strawberries
400ml light red wine
100–130g caster sugar, to taste
1 vanilla pod, split lengthways
1 cinnamon stick

FOR THE CINNAMON TOAST
flour, for dusting
250g shop-bought or homemade
    puff pastry
1 large free-range egg, beaten
1 tsp ground cinnamon
a pinch of sea salt

Rinse and hull the strawberries. In a saucepan, bring the wine, sugar,
vanilla pod and cinnamon to a gentle boil. Drop the strawberries in,
bring to the boil and immediately remove from the heat and cover. Set
aside until the wine and strawberries have cooled. At this stage the
fruit should be perfectly poached, soft yet still holding their shape.

For the cinnamon toast, roll out the pastry on a floured surface into two
rectangles about 5mm thick and chill in the fridge on a baking sheet.
Remove and brush one rectangle with some of the beaten egg and
scatter over the cinnamon. Sprinkle lightly with sea salt. Cover with
the second layer of pastry and push together. Prick all over with a fork,
brush with more egg and chill for another 20 minutes.

Meanwhile, preheat the oven to 200°C/400°F/Gas 6.

Cut the pastry into 1cm fingers and bake in the preheated oven for
10–15 minutes until golden. Remove and let cool slightly. Serve warm
with the poached strawberries.

SUMMER FRUIT GRATIN

Don't be put off by the 'gratin' element. This dish is simple, delicious
and quite startlingly beautiful. You will have some meringue and custard
left over because it is difficult to make them in smaller quantities.
But they will keep well in the fridge for a few days, so can be used for
another dish.

SERVES 4-6

500ml milk
1 vanilla pod, split lengthways
6 medium free-range egg yolks
100g caster sugar
75g plain flour
8 medium free-range egg whites
lemon juice
1 splash dark rum, brandy or
   eau de vie
400–500g summer fruit
   (nectarines, strawberries,
   raspberries, peaches,
   redcurrants, or any other
   fruits and berries you prefer,
   free from stones)

Put the milk in a saucepan with the vanilla pod, heat through gently,
and set aside to infuse.

In a bowl, whisk the egg yolks and 75g of the sugar together until pale.
Tip in the flour and stir to make a paste, then whisk in the warm,
strained milk. Return the mix to the stove, and stir until thickened and
there's no trace of flour. Set aside.

Preheat the grill.

Put the egg whites in a large clean bowl, add a squeeze of lemon juice
and beat them until they treble in size, adding the remaining sugar
(they should hold their own weight, and look like a glossy meringue).

Take a large spoon of the custard mix and throw in a dash of your
chosen booze, and then fold in most of the meringue to desire,
pillowy consistency. Use the remaining custard in another recipe (see
introduction).

Scatter the soft fruits onto a plate and spoon over the gratin mix. Place
under a scorching hot grill, or attack with a blowtorch, until the gratin
has turned golden brown on the peaks, and the mixture does not move
about when gently shaken. Serve immediately.

PAIN PERDU WITH DAMSONS AND CLOTTED CREAM

Poached damsons yield the most beautiful colour when cooked, and their tartness sits well with the sweetness of the fried toast. The cooking liquor left over makes the most delicious sorbet.

SERVES 4

250ml rich fruity red wine
finely grated zest and juice
 of 1 unwaxed orange
1 cinnamon stick
150g caster sugar
1kg fresh damsons, cut in half
 and stoned
clotted cream, to serve

FOR THE PAIN PERDU
1 brioche loaf or fruity panettone,
 sliced about 1cm thick
3 medium free-range eggs, beaten
sugar, to sprinkle
ground allspice or mixed spice
50g salted butter

In a saucepan, bring the wine, orange zest and juice, the cinnamon stick and about 125g of the sugar to the boil. Remove and pour over the damsons. If the damsons were ripe, simply cover and leave to soften; if they are still a bit hard, cook gently in the juices for 5–10 minutes. Taste and add more sugar if necessary.

For the pain perdu, dip the bread into the bowl of beaten eggs, then sprinkle with some sugar and a pinch of the allspice on both sides. Meanwhile, add the butter to a frying pan and then pan-fry the bread in gently foaming butter until golden brown on both sides.

Serve the damsons spooned over the pain perdu with a spoonful of clotted cream.

WELSH FRUIT CAKE WITH LAVENDER HONEY AND ROASTED FIGS

Teisen Lap is a very traditional spiced, moist fruit cake from Wales. Use the best figs you can find, from Provence, Italy or Greece. Leave the Brazilian ones well alone! For the lavender honey, simply infuse a good-quality honey with a small bunch (3–4 sprigs) of dried lavender to taste. Leave to mature in the jar, then use as you would plain honey.

SERVES 4-6

FOR THE FRUIT CAKE
300g sultanas
300ml strong tea (Earl Grey is good)
385g unsalted butter, plus extra for greasing
385g caster sugar
6 medium free-range eggs
385g self-raising flour
3 generous tsp mixed spice
finely grated zest of 1 unwaxed orange and 1 unwaxed lemon

FOR THE ROAST FIGS
12 ripe black or green fresh figs
50g unsalted butter, softened
300–400ml good-quality lavender honey (see introduction)

TO SERVE
lavender honey
clotted cream
8–10 sprigs dried lavender

Preheat the oven to 180°C/350°F/Gas 4. Grease and line a 25 x 35cm baking tray.

Soak the sultanas in the freshly brewed tea and set aside.

In a large bowl, cream the butter and sugar together until white and fluffy. In a separate bowl, whisk the eggs. Very slowly add the egg to the creamed butter and sugar, adding 1 tablespoon of the flour to prevent splitting. Fold in the rest of the flour and the mixed spice, and finally fold in the drained sultanas and the citrus zest. Transfer into the prepared baking tin and bake for about 1 hour or until a sharp knife inserted into the middle comes out clean. Remove from the oven and turn the temperature up to 200°C/400°F/Gas 6.

Put the figs in an ovenproof dish and simply cut across from the tip of the fig downwards three-quarters of the way and pinch open. Dot with the butter and drizzle with the lavender honey. Roast in the oven with a splash of water for 10 minutes or until the figs are just about to collapse.

Serve the Teisen Lap warm, sliced into squares, with a couple of whole roasted figs on top. Drizzle with some more lavender honey and add a dollop of clotted cream. Decorate with sprigs of dried lavender.

Photographed overleaf

CHOCOLATE POTS

These are great if you want an easy pudding to prepare in advance, and very minimal effort when you are ready to serve. These can be eaten with the orange shortbread – see opposite.

**FILLS ABOUT EIGHT
150ML POTS OR SMALL
COFFEE CUPS**

300g good-quality dark chocolate,
    at least 70% cocoa solids
500ml double cream
200ml milk
100g icing sugar
6 medium free-range or organic
    egg yolks, very fresh

TO SERVE
whipped double cream
good-quality cocoa powder
orange shortbread (see opposite),
    optional

Break the chocolate into pieces and put in a bowl. In a saucepan, boil the cream and pour over the broken-up chocolate. Stir to melt.

Combine the milk, icing sugar and egg yolks in another bowl. Pour the chocolate mix into the yolks. Stir and combine, then sieve out any egg threads. Strain into suitable pots or coffee cups and allow to set in the fridge overnight.

Serve with some whipped double cream on top and a sprinkling of cocoa powder, and the orange shortbread, if liked.

ORANGE SHORTBREAD

This recipe also works well with some finely chopped crystallised ginger
folded into the flour. Serve with the chocolate pots opposite, if you like.

MAKES 10–12 BISCUITS

120g salted butter
60g caster sugar, plus extra
    for dusting
finely grated zest of 3 unwaxed
    oranges
120g plain flour
60g polenta flour

In a bowl, beat the butter and sugar together until pale. Stir in the
orange zest. Fold in the flours and stop folding when the mix comes
together. Roll into a log about 4cm in diameter, wrap in clingfilm and
chill for 30 minutes.

Preheat the oven to 160°C/325°F/Gas 3.

Remove the shortbread dough and cut into discs about 5mm thick, then
dust with more caster sugar. (The mix can be re-rolled if necessary, but
no more than once or it will start to look greasy.) Put on a baking tray
and bake for 15–20 minutes until very pale with a slightly golden edge.

Remove, cool and serve with the chocolate pots.

POACHED CHERRY PAVLOVA, VANILLA CREAM AND TOASTED PISTACHIOS

I love the combination of sweet and sour in this pudding, and the sprinkling of pistachios adds an unexpected sweet crunchiness at the end of each mouthful. The meringue mixture makes quite a lot, but it is difficult to do in lesser quantities. Any leftovers can be broken up into whipped double cream and mixed together to make a 'fool'.

SERVES 4-6

50g shelled pistachios
2 tbsp icing sugar
300ml double cream
1 vanilla pod, split lengthways

**FOR THE CHERRIES
IN STOCK SYRUP**
200ml water
125g caster sugar
pared zest of ½ unwaxed orange
1 cinnamon stick, halved
400g fresh cherries
Kirsch (optional)

FOR THE PAVLOVA
4 medium free-range egg whites
225g caster sugar
1 tsp cornflour
½ tsp vanilla extract
1 tsp white wine vinegar
75g dried sour cherries,
    roughly chopped

Preheat the oven to 130°C/260°F/Gas ¾.

For the cherry stock syrup, put all the ingredients except for the cherries and Kirsch in a non-reactive pan, and cook until the sugar has just dissolved. Remove the stones and stalks from two-thirds of the cherries. Poach all the cherries in the sugar syrup until just tender, about 10 minutes. Add a big splash of Kirsch to this, if liked. Allow to cool in the liquid.

Toast the pistachio nuts with the icing sugar in a non-stick pan, then tip out onto a piece of non-stick baking paper and leave to cool before roughly chopping. Reserve.

While the cherries are cooling, take a ladle of the poaching liquid and reduce to a semi-sticky syrup consistency in a separate pan. This will garnish the dish when served and add a greater depth of flavour.

To make the pavlova, in a mixer whisk up the egg whites and sugar to stiff peaks. This will take between 20 and 30 minutes, or until the sugar has completely dissolved. Throw in the cornflour, vanilla extract and white wine vinegar, and fold together with the dried sour cherries.

Dollop or pipe the pavlova mixture onto non-stick baking mats in individual portion sizes – they will expand, so about a tablespoon per person. Cook in the preheated oven for about 30 minutes, or until they lift off the non-stick mat cleanly.

Meanwhile, whip the double cream with the scraped seeds of the vanilla pod, and a splash of Kirsch if using, to semi-stiff peaks – just until it holds its own weight.

Spoon a generous amount of the vanilla cream onto each pavlova and drizzle over the stoned poached cherries and the reduced sauce. Scatter over the pistachios and decorate with the whole cherries.

ESPRESSO AND
PECAN BROWNIE

This was one of the most popular puddings on the menu at our restaurant. And it is more of a pudding than a cake, as there's no flour. Keeping it slightly molten ensures a delicious texture. It works really well with walnuts too, or no nuts at all.

SERVES 8–10 GENEROUSLY

170g unsalted butter
200g shelled pecans, chopped
300g good dark chocolate, broken into pieces
150g soft brown sugar
4 medium free-range eggs
100g raisins, softened in a hot double espresso
150g mascarpone cheese
1 shot espresso or strong filter coffee

Preheat the oven to 150°C/300°F/Gas 2.

Melt 20g of the butter and use it to line a 30cm cake tin, or suitable dish. Grind a handful of the pecans and put them in the tin too, sticking to the butter. This prevents the cake from sticking.

Melt the chocolate over a bowl of simmering water. In an electric mixer, blend the remaining butter and the sugar until pale. Slowly add each egg, alternating with the drained raisins and the rest of the pecans. At this point the mix will look like it's horribly split, but don't panic because it will all come together when the chocolate is added. Beat in the mascarpone and coffee shot. Finally, add the chocolate and fold together.

Pour into the prepared tin and bake in the preheated oven for 25–30 minutes or until a crack appears round the inside surface. Allow to cool to room temperature.

Serve with maple syrup ice cream (see opposite).

MAPLE SYRUP ICE CREAM

The perfect accompaniment for the espresso and pecan brownie
opposite. Make sure you use a good-quality syrup, as many 'maple-
flavoured syrups' are imitations and usually have little or no real maple
syrup content.

SERVES 8-10 (WITH
THE BROWNIE)

300ml good maple syrup
300ml milk
1 vanilla pod, split lengthways
5 medium free-range egg yolks
450ml double cream

Put the maple syrup in a saucepan and reduce by half. In another
saucepan, heat the milk and vanilla pod, bringing them to the boil
3 times to infuse. In a bowl, whisk the yolks until light and pale.

Pour the strained hot milk over the yolks, mix and pour back into a
clean pan. Thicken on a gentle heat until the custard coats the back
of a spoon. Immediately pour in the double cream and reduced maple
syrup. Sieve and churn in an ice-cream machine, or freeze in a
suitable container. This ice cream will never set completely: due to the
extremely high sugar content, it will always remain quite soft.

TRADITIONAL CUSTARD

This is more akin to the thick custard I grew up on as a child. I still
prefer this richer, thicker variety to the more fashionable crème
anglaise served in restaurants.

MAKES ABOUT 500ML

250ml milk
250ml double cream
2 vanilla pods, split lengthways,
    seeds scraped
8 medium free-range egg yolks
100g light brown sugar
3 tbsp cornflour, slaked with
    a little water

In a saucepan, boil the milk with the cream and the vanilla.

Beat together the yolks and sugar. Add the cornflour and water to the
yolks. Pour the hot milk and cream mixture onto the yolks, and stir.
Cook gently, stirring constantly, for 5–10 minutes to make sure you've
killed off any floury taste.

The thickening will happen quite quickly but the floury taste will take a
bit longer to lose. (Make sure the custard doesn't catch at this stage or
it will acquire an unpleasant, smoky taste.)

Serve hot with a traditional British sponge pudding or baked
seasonal fruits.

STOLLEN WITH HONEY BUTTER

I love marzipan in anything but it does conjure up Christmas for me.
This particular recipe also uses cranberries and clementines
for the very same reason.

SERVES 6-8

FOR THE STOLLEN
100g unsalted butter, cubed
300g strong white flour, plus
    extra for dusting
½ tsp salt
150ml whole milk, plus extra
    to glaze
60g caster sugar
7g dried yeast
3 clementines, zested
100g dried cranberries, chopped
50g pecan nuts, chopped
60g dark chocolate chunks
200g marzipan, rolled into a
    long log

FOR THE HONEY BUTTER
100g unsalted butter, room
    temperature
60g clear honey
10g icing sugar

To make the loaf, rub the butter into the flour and salt in a large mixing bowl to make a breadcrumb consistency.

Heat the milk in a small pan to blood temperature, add the sugar and the yeast and mix well. Then add the grated clementine zest, cranberries, pecans and chocolate to the breadcrumb mix. Make a well in the centre and add the warmed milk. Mix to a soft dough.

Knead the dough for 10 minutes on a lightly floured surface before rolling it into a rectangle of 30 x 15cm. Roll the marzipan to a length that will fit the loaf and lay it down one edge. Roll the dough over to encase the marzipan – you can brush the edges with a little water to help them seal. Arrange on a baking tray lined with greaseproof paper, cover and leave to prove for 30 minutes in a warm place.

Preheat the oven to 160°C/325°F/Gas 3. Brush the loaf with milk to glaze and bake for 45–60 minutes. Remove from the oven, cover with a clean tea towel and allow to cool a bit before slicing.

To make the honey butter, beat the butter until soft in a bowl, add the honey and icing sugar, and beat again until soft and smooth. To serve, slice the loaf and spread with the honey butter.

COFFEE CAKE, MASCARPONE AND VANILLA CREAM

My mother makes this cake for me every year around Christmas and over the years it has become my all-time favourite. It is a bit tiramisu-like but simpler to prepare. I think it's utterly delicious, and why it's been confined to an outing once a year, I have no idea!

SERVES 8–10

125g salted butter, plus extra
  for greasing
125g caster sugar
2 large free-range eggs, beaten
225g self-raising flour
1 tsp bicarbonate of soda
400ml water
175g caster sugar
5 tbsp coffee essence or
  good-quality strong coffee
6–8 tbsp brandy, or to taste

**FOR THE MASCARPONE
AND VANILLA CREAM**
250g mascarpone cheese
1 medium free-range egg yolk
1–2 tbsp icing sugar, to taste
1 vanilla pod, split lengthways
  and seeds scraped (or 1 tsp
  vanilla extract)
125g double cream

Preheat the oven to 160°C/325°F/Gas 3. Grease a 23cm springform cake tin.

In a large bowl, cream the butter and sugar together until pale. Gradually add the beaten eggs. Carefully fold in the flour and bicarb, then spoon the mixture into the prepared tin. Bake in the preheated oven for 35–45 minutes. Remove and cool for a while, still in the tin.

Meanwhile, in a pan, heat together the water, sugar, coffee essence and brandy, just until the sugar has dissolved. When the cake is still warm, prick it all over with a skewer or fork, to better absorb the coffee and brandy mixture which you spoon over the top.

Just before serving, make the mascarpone cream. Mix the mascarpone with the egg yolk and icing sugar to taste. Stir in the vanilla seeds and double cream.

Remove the cake from its tin. Serve the soaked cake warm, in slices, with the mascarpone and vanilla cream.

GINGERBREAD CAKES

The French call these nonnettes, 'little nuns', after the Dijon nuns who invented them. They are deliciously moreish, muffin-sized gingerbread cakes made with honey and spices.

MAKES 6

80g salted butter, plus extra
    for greasing
200ml honey
100ml milk
90g dark brown sugar
250g plain flour
50g rye flour
2 tsp baking powder
1 tsp bicarbonate of soda
a pinch of ground cinnamon
a few twists of black pepper
a pinch of ground cloves
a pinch of ground ginger
a pinch of freshly grated nutmeg
a pinch of mace
150g marmalade

TO SERVE
fine orange zest
icing sugar

Preheat the oven to 200°C/400°F/Gas 6 and grease a 6-hole muffin tin.

Mix the butter, honey, milk, sugar and 100ml water together in a pan over a medium heat to dissolve the sugar and melt the butter.

In a large bowl, sift the flours with the baking powder, bicarbonate of soda and spices.

Stir the melted liquid mixture into the flour and spices while still warm and mix well. Fill the muffin holes halfway, then add a spoon of marmalade and top up each hole with the remaining mixture. Bake for 20 minutes.

Remove and let cool. Sprinkle over the orange zest and dust with icing sugar to serve.

CHRISTMAS PANETTONE TRIFLE

Panettone has become a popular gift in this country at Christmas.
I often find myself with a few in the house. It is light and fruity so
it makes a perfect trifle base. This recipe uses dried fruit instead
of fresh or tinned, to give it a rich, Christmas-pudding feel.

SERVES 8

FOR THE CHRISTMAS FRUITS
100g Medjool dates, stoned
100g prunes
100g dried apricots
100g candied peel
100g dried cranberries
100g raisins
zest and juice of 1 unwaxed orange
100g pecan nuts, chopped
100g whole almonds, chopped
1 cinnamon stick
½ nutmeg, grated
½ tsp ground mixed spice
750ml Marsala

FOR THE TRIFLE FILLING
2 free-range eggs, separated
100g icing sugar
50ml Marsala
500g good-quality ricotta, such
    as Westcombe

TO ASSEMBLE
1 panettone
100ml Marsala
2–3 clementines, peeled and
    segmented
Seeds of 1 pomegranate
400ml custard (see page 207)
100g pistachio slivers

Preheat the oven to 160°C/325°F/Gas 3.

Place all the Christmas fruits ingredients into an ovenproof dish with a
lid and pour the Marsala over. Bake in the oven with the lid on for
3 hours. Add some water if necessary, to stop it drying out.

To make the trifle filling, in a bowl, beat the egg yolks with the icing
sugar until thick and pale. Add the Marsala and ricotta and mix well.

Whisk the egg whites in a separate bowl until stiff peaks form when
the whisk is removed from the bowl. Fold the egg whites through the
Marsala and ricotta mixture.

To assemble the trifle, cut the panettone to fit the size of your trifle
serving dish (preferably made of glass). Douse with the Marsala and
top with some of the cooled, cooked fruits and some of the clementines
and pomegranate seeds. Spoon over a layer of the custard and then
the ricotta cream. Repeat the layers again to build up the trifle.
Finish with the pistachio slivers and more pomegranate seeds for
decoration. Serve.

AMARETTI BISCUITS

These biscuits are the chewy variety of amaretti, and keep well for
several days in an airtight box.

MAKES 50~60

4 medium free-range egg whites,
   very fresh
560g icing sugar, plus extra
   for dusting
a pinch of salt
1 tsp almond essence
450g ground almonds
a handful of flaked almonds

Preheat the oven to 150°C/300°F/Gas 2.

Put two of the egg whites into a food mixer with half the sugar. Mix with
the blade attachment, not the whisk — you don't want to fill the biscuits
with too much air. Add the pinch of salt, the almond essence, the
ground almonds, the rest of the sugar and the remaining egg whites.
The consistency should be thick enough to roll.

Dust a worktop with icing sugar and roll out the dough. Roll it into a
sausage about 1cm in diameter. Slice the roll into individual 2.5cm
pieces, and flatten them lightly on greased baking trays. Add the flaked
almonds, sticking them randomly on the top.

Cook in the preheated oven for 30–40 minutes until the biscuits are
firm and can be removed from the tray easily. They should be lightly
golden in colour. Dust with more icing sugar and serve warm.

HAZELNUT SHORTBREADS

If you like, you can substitute other nuts for the hazelnuts, and a handful
of raisins thrown into the mix is also good. These biscuits are easy and
quick to make, and sturdy enough to keep in an airtight container for a
few days.

**MAKES AS MANY OR FEW
AS YOU LIKE, DEPENDING
ON SIZE**

300g shelled hazelnuts
300g unsalted butter, plus extra
    for greasing
250g light brown sugar
350g plain flour
a pinch of ground allspice
icing sugar, to dust

Preheat the oven to 180°C/350°F/Gas 4 and grease a large baking tray.

Toast the hazelnuts in a dry frying pan until golden, and then blitz in a
food processor.

Blend the butter and sugar together in a bowl, then mix in the flour,
allspice and the blitzed hazelnuts.

Shape however desired on the prepared baking tray. I make these into
quenelles using 2 dessertspoons, but they will taste just as good shaped
into small rounds. Cook in the preheated oven for 10–15 minutes until
golden brown.

Remove, cool on a wire rack and dust with icing sugar before serving.

BASICS & PRESERVES

VEGETABLE STOCK

This is a great way of putting vegetable trimmings and excess veg
to good use!

MAKES ABOUT 1.4 LITRES

2 white onions, peeled and
  quartered
2 fennel bulbs
2 leeks
1 head of celery, diced
a handful of parsley stalks
1 garlic bulb, cut in half
1 tsp white peppercorns
1 tsp coriander seeds
a few sprigs aromatic herbs, such
  as tarragon or chervil
a few bay leaves
1.5 litres cold water

Put all the ingredients into a large saucepan, and bring to the boil.
Skim and simmer at the merest blip for about 25 minutes. Strain
and cool.

Store in the fridge for no more than a day to ensure its freshness.

WHITE FISH STOCK

For fish stock, use only white fish bones, not oily, such as salmon or mackerel. Veal or beef stock can be made in the same way, with the same quantity of relevant bones, but with a much longer cooking time. On the whole, beef or veal stock should be cooked for no less than 8 hours. The veal bones could be roasted (as in the lamb stock recipe, page 224) to make a dark as opposed to a light veal stock.

MAKES ABOUT 2 LITRES

3kg white fish bones
2 leeks, cleaned and diced
2 white onions, peeled and diced
1 fennel bulb, roughly sliced
1 garlic bulb
3–4 bay leaves
1 head of celery, diced
a handful of parsley stalks

Wash the bones, cover with water in a large saucepan and bring to the boil.

Skim off any impurities and fat, then top up with more cold water. Add the vegetables and aromatics: the water should cover everything. Bring to the boil, skim once more, then simmer, uncovered, for 20–30 minutes, but no more.

Sieve and store in the fridge or freezer. (Fish stock kept in a fridge will keep for no longer than two to three days.)

CHICKEN STOCK

You could make a duck or guinea fowl stock in exactly the same way.

MAKES ABOUT 2 LITRES

3.5kg chicken carcasses, and wings
   if possible
1 head of celery, halved
2 white onions, peeled and halved
3 carrots, halved
2 leeks, cleaned and halved
2 garlic bulbs, halved
3–4 bay leaves
½ bunch fresh thyme
1 tsp black peppercorns

Put the bones, on their own, into a large saucepan. Add enough cold water to cover the bones and bring to the boil. Skim off all the impurities that rise to the surface. Replace the removed water with more cold water. Bring this back to the boil and skim again.

Now add the veg and aromatics, and bring back to the boil. Reduce the heat and simmer, uncovered, for about 3 hours, skimming occasionally.

Pass through a fine sieve and refrigerate or freeze. This will keep in the fridge for a week and in the freezer for many months.

LAMB STOCK

I like to make my own lamb stock if I have time, as it's more flavoursome
than chicken stock and it makes a much better gravy.

MAKES ABOUT 2 LITRES

3kg lamb bones
1 head of celery, halved
2 white onions, peeled and halved
3 carrots, halved
2 leeks, cleaned and halved
2 garlic bulbs, halved
100ml vegetable oil
1 tbsp tomato purée
1 tsp black peppercorns
2 sprigs rosemary
3–4 bay leaves

Preheat the oven to 180°C/350°F/Gas 4.

Brown the lamb bones in a roasting tin in the oven until golden brown.
This will take 30–40 minutes.

In a large saucepan, sauté the veg in the oil until browned, about 25–30
minutes. Stir in the tomato purée and cook for 5 minutes. Add the lamb
bones and aromatics.

Add enough cold water to cover everything and bring to the boil. Skim
off the impurities and fat. Reduce the heat and simmer, uncovered, for
about 2 hours.

Put through a sieve and refrigerate until needed. The stock will keep
for a week in the fridge and a few months in the freezer.

HORSERADISH CREAM SAUCE

This is a hot and piquant sauce to accompany venison, beef or even salmon. A good spoonful of crème fraîche stirred in at the end adds a slight sour note.

SERVES 8-10

½ white onion, peeled and diced
1 garlic clove, peeled and crushed
25g unsalted butter
125ml dry white wine, or to taste
150ml chicken stock (see page 222)
500ml double cream
80g freshly grated horseradish
salt and pepper

In a saucepan, sweat the onion and garlic off in the butter until soft but not browned. Add the dry white wine and reduce by half. Add the stock and reduce by half again.

Add the cream and bring to the boil. Take off the heat, strain if desired and stir in the horseradish. Season and serve.

PINEAPPLE CHUTNEY

This is super easy to make and keeps for a month or more in the fridge. It's the perfect accompaniment to roast gammon, pork or other cooked meats.

SERVES 4 AS AN ACCOMPANIMENT

2 white onions, peeled and diced
   into small chunks
50ml olive oil
1 tsp brown mustard seeds, toasted
salt and pepper
1 garlic clove, peeled and
   finely sliced
1 pineapple, peeled and cut
   into chunks
1 sprig fresh rosemary
1 tbsp (floral) honey
100ml cider vinegar
120g light brown sugar
50g blanched almonds, toasted

In a saucepan, sweat off the onions in the olive oil for 10–15 minutes. Add the mustard seeds and season. Add the garlic, followed by the remainder of the ingredients, and stir.

Gently stew down for 1 hour or more until a jammy consistency. Adjust the acidity – adding a touch more brown sugar if necessary – and season accordingly.

CHILLI AND TOMATO CHUTNEY

The chilli seeds make this chutney pretty hot, so remove them if you prefer something milder. Serve with a good strong Cheddar.

MAKES 1 LITRE

1 large onion, peeled and
   finely chopped
50ml olive oil
5 tsp finely grated garlic
3 tsp finely grated fresh ginger
6 fresh red chillies, roasted,
   skinned and chopped
3 tsp yellow mustard seeds, toasted
1kg canned tomatoes, or 1kg ripe
   fresh tomatoes, skinned
250g caster sugar dissolved in 250g
   white wine vinegar
salt

In a saucepan, fry the onion in the olive oil for 10 minutes to soften, then throw in the garlic and ginger and cook for a further 5 minutes.

Add the chopped chilli (seeds and flesh), and throw in the mustard seeds and tomatoes. Stew down for 20 minutes until most of the liquid has evaporated.

Add the sugar and vinegar solution and bring back to the boil. Season with salt, remove from the heat and allow to cool. Store in the fridge.

GRILLED FLATBREADS

This will make more than enough, but the dough is pretty good turned
into a focaccia bread or even a quick pizza base. It keeps very well in the
fridge for a few days.

SERVES 4-6

15g fresh yeast
2–3 tbsp lukewarm water
500g strong bread flour
½ tsp salt
1 tbsp olive oil
10 tbsp water, plus extra if needed

TO SERVE
olive oil
sea salt

Crumble the yeast into a bowl, then whisk in the lukewarm water. Sift
the flour and salt into a separate bowl. Make a well in the middle.

Pour the yeast water into the well in the flour and add the olive oil and
10 tablespoons water. Mix to form a dough. Add another tablespoon or
more of water, if necessary, to make it nice and workable. Knead the
dough until it is soft and pliable, about 10 minutes.

Place the dough in a bowl, cover loosely and leave to prove in a warm
place for a few hours. Remove the dough from the bowl and knead
lightly to knock back, about 5 minutes. Cover and leave in the fridge.

When required, rip a small amount of dough off and roll out into disc
shapes, roughly the size of a small saucer, allowing one per person.

Chargrill or throw on a very hot dry frying pan for 1–2 minutes each
side until charred and cooked through.

Drizzle with olive oil and sprinkle with sea salt to serve.

TARTARE SAUCE

It sounds a little strange to serve tartare sauce with meat, but the
piquancy of the sauce works beautifully with the fatty richness of meat.
This mayonnaise develops as it is left in the fridge. It will keep quite
happily for a few days.

SERVES 4

3 medium free-range egg yolks
1 garlic clove, peeled and crushed
1 tsp Dijon mustard
salt and pepper
200ml salad oil (half vegetable,
  half olive)
1 squeeze lemon juice
1 tbsp baby capers
1 tbsp chopped gherkins or
  cornichons
1 tsp chopped fresh tarragon

Mayonnaise, in my opinion, must be made by hand, or it will always
look shop-bought.

Whisk the egg yolks in a bowl. Mix in the crushed garlic and Dijon
mustard with a pinch of salt and pepper, then very slowly glug the
oil in, while whisking. Watch out that the eggs take all the oil on, and
do not separate. If at any stage the eggs look greasy, then stop, add a
squeeze of lemon juice, then continue. Whisk until the mayonnaise
is thick and creamy.

Stir the baby capers and gherkins through at the end along with
the tarragon.

CAPER MUSTARD VINAIGRETTE

Capers are a traditional match for mutton or lamb; they supply the necessary piquancy to balance the meat's richness.

SERVES 4

1 tsp baby capers
1 tbsp sherry vinegar
3 tbsp olive oil
1 tsp Dijon mustard
½ garlic clove, peeled and crushed

Mix all the ingredients together to make a vinaigrette.

INDEX

ABOUT THE AUTHOR

Matt Tebbutt is a TV presenter and chef, who presents BBC TV's long-running flagship food show, *Saturday Kitchen*. He has also presented *Food Unwrapped* on Channel 4 for 12 years. In 2020 he was voted Fortnum & Mason Food Personality of the Year. He trained under Alastair Little, Marco Pierre White and Sally Clarke. For many years he ran his award-winning restaurant The Foxhunter in Monmouthshire.

ACKNOWLEDGEMENTS

Thanks goes out to Sarah, Sophie and Gemma and all the team at Quadrille for producing such a lovely book.

To Chris Terry and Roo Hasan for making the food look stunning as usual and for all the continuous laughs on the long shoot days.

To Hilary, Charlotte and all at Arlington for managing me so well, in more ways than one!

To the gang at Saturday Kitchen, Amanda and all the brilliant team at Cactus TV, for giving me the best job in the world, week in-week out.

To Mitch and Mat at Rockfish Seafood Market for their help with sourcing first-class produce and endless hospitality over the years.

To Rich and Cath for lending me their house in the early days and for eating all my food and never complaining!

To Rhiannon and Jason, the perfect hosts at The Halfway, Tal-y-coed. My lovely local.

To my wife Lisa, who waded through hours of illegible notes and bad spelling to bring this book to life... and without whom none of this would be possible.

And finally to my kids, Jessie and Henry, for just being ace and fun to have around. And to the rest of my brilliant family and loyal friends who have supported me so well over the years.

MANAGING DIRECTOR: SARAH LAVELLE
EDITORIAL DIRECTOR: SOPHIE ALLEN
SENIOR DESIGNER: GEMMA HAYDEN
PHOTOGRAPHER: CHRIS TERRY
FOOD STYLIST: ROO HASAN
PROP STYLIST: FAYE WEARS
HEAD OF PRODUCTION: STEPHEN LANG
PRODUCTION CONTROLLER: GARY HAYES

Published in 2024 by Quadrille Publishing Limited

Quadrille
52–54 Southwark Street
London SE1 1UN

quadrille.com

Some recipes previously published in *Matt Tebbutt Cooks Country*
(Mitchell Beazley, 2008).

ISBN 9781837831241
Printed with soy inks in China

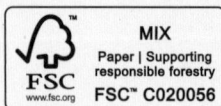

FSC
www.fsc.org
MIX
Paper | Supporting
responsible forestry
FSC™ C020056